Reproduction of chart sections
used to illustrate this
book is with the permission
of the Controller of H.M.
Stationery Office and of the
Hydrographer of the Navy

This book is based on
articles which have
previously appeared in
YACHTING & BOATING WEEKLY

Yachting & Boating Book of Navigation

CAPTAIN D. O. HARVEY, M.I.N.

SPHERE BOOKS LTD
30/32 Gray's Inn Road, London, WC1X 8JL

Cover Illustration
The first Morning Cloud
photograph by Gordon Yeldham

TRADE MARK

SPHERE

CONTENTS

Part I Coastal Navigation

Part II Astro-Navigation

FOREWORD

The majority of people, who left their maths behind them at school, believe navigation to be a science fraught with difficulties. But it is also an art which the small craft owner longs to acquire, for without it he cannot venture beyond the buoyed channels or nearest headland.

I first met Captain Harvey when he was taking an evening class of would-be navigators through the intricacies of chartwork, and was so impressed by the clear, painless way in which he brought light into darkness, that I persuaded him to write a series of lectures for YACHTING & BOATING, then a brand new weekly yachting paper. His articles were immediately successful; so much so that, within a fortnight, the Admiralty had to reprint the practice charts on which the course was based.

Now the whole course is here in book form, plus an additional section on Astro-navigation. This latter also appeared in YACHTING & BOATING, in the same author's painless style.

In these pages, in fact, navigation is proved a subject which all who sail small craft can acquire; and its acquisition is likely to have more effect on the current drive for safety at sea than is almost any other medium.

Charles F. Jones

CHAPTER ONE

LOOKING AT THE CHART

The immortal Mrs. Beeton begins her recipe for Jugged Hare with the instruction to "first catch your hare." The first thing, then, in beginning chartwork, is to get a chart.

Modern charts are the product of centuries of effort. They are accurate and dependable, and are worthy of the reverence with which they should be treated. They should be kept flat, or at the worst rolled up – never folded into small squares. And nothing should ever be put on them except the instruments used in working on them. They cost between 10s. and £1 each, but this is no measure of their value.

In case I have produced too great a feeling of inferiority in the face of such hallowed objects, let me re-assure you by telling you that the Admiralty publishes what are called "practice charts" costing only 5p each; charts which may be approached with much more freedom, used, or even abused, with impunity, but which react to kind usage by remaining legible and whole. **No. 5116.**

We will be working on the "Dover Straits" practice chart, which can be obtained from any Admiralty chart agent and no doubt from nautical booksellers. **(from 1431).**

The first part of this book constitutes a complete course on the subject of Chartwork and Pilotage, a course which, for a full time student of average ability and intelligence, might take forty-eight hours to bring him up to examination standard. This is the period required for an individual urged on by the incentives of professional advancement, more money, more comfort, and who has available personal guidance.

But since the subject involves only simple arithmetic, simple practical geometry, and the ability to memorize one rule, I am sure that those of my readers who follow the instructions and do the exercises provided will be surprised and pleased at their progress.

* * *

The Earth is round, but it can be projected on to a flat piece of paper, for our purposes, thanks to a Flemish scientist called Mercator. The first Mercator chart was published in 1569. Its principal characteristics are that the parallels of latitude (the lines running across the chart) are straight lines parallel to each other. The meridians of longitude (the vertical lines on the chart) are straight lines parallel to each other, and perpendicular to the parallels of latitude.

Since on the Earth the meridians converge towards the Poles, the fact that they are parallel on the chart means that the further one goes from the equator the greater the East-West distortion of land masses. To counteract this on the chart, the parallels of latitude, which are equally spaced on the Earth, are spaced at increasing distances on the chart to maintain the correct shape of the land.

This means that, on a Mercator chart, Greenland will be as big as Africa, whereas in fact it is not nearly so big.

Another important feature of a Mercator chart is that bearings or courses can be drawn as straight lines.

Looking at the Dover Straits chart, you will notice that the sea is full of numbers. These numbers denote the depth of water in fathoms, a fathom being six feet. This depth is measured from a level called Chart Datum to the bottom of the sea, and shows the least amount of water at each place. This is to say that, where the chart shows six fathoms, there will always be six fathoms of water, perhaps more but never less.

The contour lines in the water consisting of dots and dashes pass through places having the same depth, and conform to a very simple system. Up to 9 fathoms the lines are denoted by the number of fathoms in dots with a space between them, i.e. the five fathom line is so ····· ····· ····· etc. Above nine fathoms the ten is represented by dots, the zeros by dashes, i.e. the 10 fathom line ··-··-·· the 20 fathom line ··-··-··-·· and so on.

If you look in Somme Bay on the French coast you will see on the sand there underlined figures. These mean that when the water is at Chart Datum, this sand is that number of feet above water.

11

Going back to the soundings, it will be noted that alongside many of them are letters. These letters denote the kind of bottom, i.e. S sand, R rock, M mud, and so on. Details of all these abbreviations, along with much other information, are contained in Chart No. 5011, price 2/–, which you should also purchase.

Here and there in the water are letters of the alphabet enclosed in a diamond so ◈. These refer to the tide tables in the bottom right-hand corner of the chart. In table K is given the direction and rate of the tidal stream at K for every hour of the tide before and after High Water at Dover. The rate is given for Neap tides and Spring tides.

Spring tides occur about two days after new and full moon. Neaps midway between Spring tides; i.e. there is a Spring tide every fortnight; and a Neap tide a week after a Spring tide. (The tide rises higher and falls lower at Spring tides than at Neap tides.)

High water at Dover is about twenty minutes past eleven nearest to the time of new and full moon. If full moon is at noon, high water will be at 11.20 a.m. on that day.

There is a period of about 12 hours. 25 mins. between successive high waters, but to avoid a calculation it is as well to get a table of times of High and Low water at Dover. We will be going into the practical application of these tide tables on the chart later.

CHAPTER TWO

TRUE AND MAGNETIC

Once upon a time when we wanted to go to the four corners of the earth, we went North, South, East, or West. Not any more. Now we go 000°, 180°, 090°, or 270° respectively.

This is what is called the Three Figure Notation of Direction, and it simplifies life considerably for the navigator. The three figures are followed by a letter, i.e. 160°T, or 106°M, or 106°C.

T stands for True and means that the course or bearing is an angle in relation to the meridians on the chart. M stands for Magnetic and means that the course or bearing is the angle in relation to a meridian passing through the magnetic pole. C stands for Compass, and means that the course or bearing is taken from the compass itself.

If you look again at the chart you will find in the Dover Strait a compass rose. This consists of three graduated circles, the outer one in degrees from 000° to 359°, the middle one with its North point offset some degrees to the outer one, and the inner one divided into points and quarter points. This rose is for the purpose of finding the direction of courses and bearings laid off on the chart.

To lay off these courses and bearings, and to find their direction, we need some kind of instruments. For this purpose we can use parallel rulers, which can be bought for from 7/6d. upwards. Or we can use two set squares. Or we can use a set square and ruler. All are equally efficient in the right hands.

If you decide on set squares or a ruler, get them without bevelled edges, so that when placed edge to edge they do not ride over one another.

While we are talking about instruments, in addition to the above you will need a pair of compasses, a pair of dividers, a 2B pencil, and a rubber, for future work.

The method of using parallel rulers is, I feel, self-evident. To use set squares to find the direction of a course, lay the long side of one set square along the course on the chart, and lay one side of the other set square along one side of the first. By moving only one at a time, and sliding one along the other, towards the nearest compass rose, the long side of number one square may finally be made to pass through the centre of the rose, and the course read off where it cuts the graduations.

It will cut in two places of course, diametrically opposite one another. Make sure that you select the correct one. It is very mortifying to find that you have been coming when you should have been going.

When using a ruler and set square proceed as above, keep sliding the set square along the ruler, moving only one at a time.

Before actually embarking on some practical work, we must get clear the method of fixing the position of anything on the earth. This is done by finding its Latitude and Longitude.

The earth being round, its circumference is divided up into 180° in a North and South direction and round the equator in an East and West direction. Latitude is measured from 0° to 90° N. or S. of the equator, and Longitude from 0° to 180° E. or W. of the Greenwich meridian. On our Dover Strait chart the scale of latitude can be found down each side of the margin.

Notice that the parallel of 51°N. runs across just north of Calais.

Each degree is divided into 60 minutes, and further down the margin the figure 50 denotes the number of minutes; in this case, above the next degree south of 51, i.e. 50°50 N., the parallel of 50°N. being just off the chart to the southward.

On the earth the minutes of latitude are the same length anywhere. One minute is equal to one nautical mile, so that distance on the chart is always measured on the latitude scale 1′ equals one nautical mile. The nautical mile differs in length from the statute mile, but since one is measured on land and the other at sea there is no problem here.

The average nautical mile is 6080 feet, call it 6000 feet, for

14

after all what is 80 feet as long as you don't have to swim it? One tenth of this is 600 feet or 200 yards and is called in nautical terms a cable.

You will notice on the latitude scale that each minute is divided up into five parts, 0.2 of a mile, or 2 cables. When measuring distance on a Mercator chart, it should always be measured on that part of the latitude scale abreast of the distance measured, because by its method of construction, the scale of the chart increases as the latitude increases.

At the top and bottom of the chart is the longitude scale. Note the meridian of 1°E runs just eastwards of Dungeness. The length of 1° of longitude is different from 1° of latitude except on the equator, so the longitude scale is only used for measuring longitude. The length of 1° longitude in latitude 60 is exactly half the length of 1° of latitude. This fact is merely of interest, for we only use the longitude scale to find our longitude.

Many people complain that they cannot learn from books. There are several reasons for this. You are working on your own without encouragement, without anyone to help with additional explanation when the going gets tough, and you come to a point which you don't understand. In a class, this does not arise, since you are one student among several. Besides, there is a teacher present to show you what to do and explain how and why.

Also, there are too many distractions at home for you to be able to concentrate, or you may not be able to find time for such a frivolous subject as chartwork, and so on.

In my time, I have learned a great deal from books, and this is the method. Never expect to understand what a book says the first time you read it.

You have to read everything several times before you really understand it. This is not because you are stupid, but simply because the subject is new and you have to get into its groove.

You must take everything bit by bit. When you get lost go back again to where you left the track and try again.

Do one thing at a time, and understand it before going on.

It is better to learn one thing too much than two things not enough.

In this particular subject we are fortunate in that it is composed of short processes, each of which can be explained in a paragraph. I propose to explain them as if to the most limited intelligence, so bear with me in this. You will be able to practise these processes in the train on a piece of scrap paper, or on your chart at home – and you will be amazed at how easy it is after a while to navigate a vessel all over the Channel.

I must point out, however, before we get carried away, that it is not quite so cut and dried when actually at sea in these parts. But at least you will learn how to go about it in theory, and then you will be able to put the theory into practice.

Before we go any farther, however, you must have a chart and some instruments. We will then be able to begin something practical.

CHAPTER THREE

GETTING DOWN TO CHARTWORK

To find the Latitude and Longitude of a given position on the chart, measure with the dividers the distance in a N-S direction to the nearest parallel of Latitude, and transfer this distance to the scale at the side of the chart.

Or place the parallel rulers along a parallel, and then shift one edge through the position so that it cuts the scale at the side of the chart, where the Latitude may be read off.

The Longitude may be found by measuring the E-W distance to the nearest meridian and transferring this distance to the scale at the top or bottom of the chart, or –

By using the parallel rulers as above, but this time first placing them along a meridian.

Meridians of Longitude run North and South, parallels of Latitude run East and West.

Presumably you now have the practice chart, so find the Latitude and Longitude of the following places:

Beachy Head Light Ho., Paris Plage Gp. Fl. Light., Folkestone Gp. Fl. Light.

To plot a position described by its Latitude and Longitude place the parallel rules along a parallel of Latitude and move them so that one edge passes through the given Latitude on the scale at the side of the chart. Now measure the Longitude on the scale at the top or bottom of the chart from the nearest meridian, using the dividers, and lay this off from the same meridian along the edge of the rulers passing through the Latitude.

Now plot the following positions on the chart and say what you find there:

Lat. 50° 48.4′N.   Lat. 50° 52.8′N.
Long. 1° 12′E.   Long. 0° 30.9′E.
              Lat. 50° 59.6′N.
              Long. 0° 55.2′E.

The position of anything, particularly a ship, may be described by its bearing and distance from some object. On the titles of many charts it says "All bearings are true and are given from seaward." This refers to such things as the coloured sectors of lights from lighthouses, or bearings for clearing marks.

In practice, however, in giving a position it is as well to

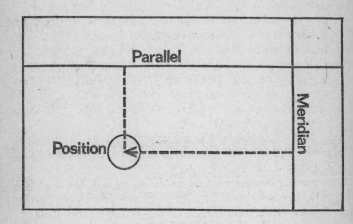

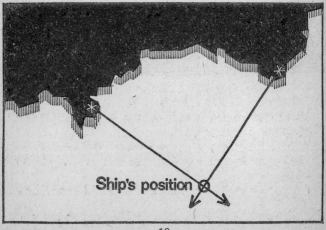

specify strictly whether the bearing is from or of the object, i.e. "Bearing 106 T. from Beachy Head Light, distant 4 mls." or "Beachy Head Light bearing 286 T, distant 4 mls." These two statements refer to the same position, as you will notice.

It would be most upsetting if you were in the water three miles south of the Royal Sovereign Light Vessel, and the lifeboat was looking for you three miles north of it, just because you had given an ambiguous reference. Let us hope that you will never be in such a case, but be prepared!

To plot the above position with reference to Beachy Head Light, lay one edge of the parallel rules through the centre of the nearest compass rose so that it cuts the outer ring at either 286° or 106°, and then transfer one edge of the rules until it passes through Beachy Head Light.

Take a distance of 4 mls. on the dividers, and measure it off along the ruler from the Light, making sure that it is laid off in the correct direction.

In order to find our position at any time, it is necessary to obtain position lines from bearings of landmarks. A position line is a line drawn on the chart which passes through the ship's position. It is obtained by taking a bearing by the compass of a known object, converting the bearing from Compass to True, and laying it off on the chart through the position of the known object.

At present we will confine ourselves to True bearings only, so that we can concentrate on one thing at a time.

The simplest and most certain method of obtaining a fix is by simultaneous bearings of two objects, laid off on the chart so that they cross at a point. The nearer the difference between the two bearings is to 90° the better. It is obvious that if the vessel is on each of these bearings she must be at the point where they cross.

Now find the position in Latitude and Longitude from each of the following sets of cross bearings, working on the chart.

(1) Dungeness Lt. bearing 253° T., Folkestone Lt. bearing 343° T.

(2) C. d'Alprech Lt. bearing 136° T., C. Gris Nez Lt. bear-

ing 074° T. Answers to all these questions are given in the Appendix.

It is not necessary to draw the complete bearings on the chart as I have done, but only the bits where they cross. The fewer the marks you put on the chart, the better.

The position obtained by the method described above is shown on the chart by a dot with a small circle drawn round it, and having the time alongside it thus: ⊙ Fix 0920.

CHAPTER FOUR

LAYING OFF A COURSE

The next thing to do is to decide where you want to go, and to lay off the course or courses to your destination – deciding how far off each turning point you must pass, and being careful to see that each course is clear of rocks, wrecks or other obstructions.

The direction of each course is taken from the True compass rose, and the distance on each course measured off the scale of Latitude at the side of the chart.

The course is taken off by laying one edge of the parallel rules along the course and transferring another edge through the centre of the compass rose to cut the graduations at the course direction.

Using set squares, the long edge of one is laid along the course, and an edge of the other laid along another edge of the first. By sliding the set squares along each other, moving only one at a time, never lifting the first one, its long edge may be made to pass through the centre of the compass rose and the course read off where it cuts the graduations.

Be careful that you take off the correct direction in which you are going, and not the one diametrically opposite.

Now work the following example:

Find the True courses to steer and the distance to steam on each course from Folkestone Gp. Fl. Lt. to a point 1½ mls. 135°T from Dungeness High Lt., thence to a point 2½ mls. 180°T from the Royal Sovereign Lt. Vessel, thence to a point 4 mls. 180°T from Beachy Head Lt.

Note that the position of a Light Vessel is denoted by a small circle in the middle of its keel.

When actually sailing along these courses it is the practice to fix the position of the vessel at frequent intervals. This we do in order to see whether the vessel is making her course or not; that is, whether she is keeping to our pencil line.

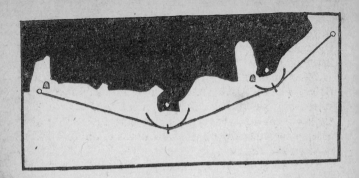

This is very unlikely, and any discrepancy between where she should be and where she is, is put down to the effect of current, wind, or bad steering!

The latter can only be remedied by paying more attention to the steering, by keeping a stricter eye on the man at the wheel. If this happens to be yourself, this will be even more difficult than if somebody else steers.

To find at any time where the vessel should be, we must know at what speed she is moving through the water. We assume that the water is not flowing, and allow the distance sailed through the water along the course steered. This gives us what is called the Dead Reckoning, or D.R. position.

To find out how far we have sailed through the water, or at what speed we are doing so, an instrument called the log is used. Logs are of various kinds, and an assortment can be seen at any chandlers. Before these modern inventions came into use, the instrument used at sea was a small triangular piece of wood with a hole near each apex, and weighted along one side, this side being convex.

Two strands of a three-stranded log line were passed through the two holes next to the weight, and knotted on the other side. The other strand was secured to a wooden peg which was pushed into the top hole. Next to the log chip (as this piece of wood was called) there was a length of stray line before the first knot.

Thereafter, at regular intervals, there were knots on the

line up to about as many as you thought you would ever do, but I can tell you that it was hard work pulling this log back on board if you were doing anything over 10 or 12 knots.

This apparatus was used with a sand glass which took either 14 or 28 seconds to run out, but in fact any number of seconds can be used. The length between two knots on the line bears the same proportion to the length of a nautical mile, as the time taken for the sand to run out to the number of seconds in an hour.

There are 6,080 feet in a nautical mile and 3,600 seconds in an hour. The length of a knot on the line is therefore found from the proportion: 3,600 : no. of seconds : : 6,080 : length of knot. For a 14 second glass the length would be 23 feet 7 inches. The length of stray line was about 12 or 15 fathoms and was intended to carry the log clear of the wake currents.

The method of finding the speed was to fix in the wooden peg and pay the log line out until the first knot crossed the rail. The log line tender then called "Turn," and the sand glass was turned upside down. The knots were counted as they crossed the rail until the sand ran out, and there was the speed. A jerk on the line released the peg and the log chip came in flat to avoid the resistance of water. Simple and effective.

A watch with a second hand could be used, or a cut

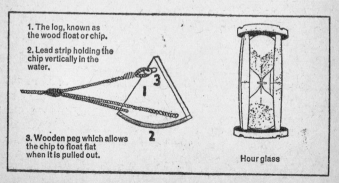

1. The log, known as the wood float or chip.

2. Lead strip holding the chip vertically in the water.

3. Wooden peg which allows the chip to float flat when it is pulled out.

Hour glass

down egg timer. Before measuring the knots on the line, it should be wetted and stretched.

There is an even simpler type of log called the Dutchman's log, with all due apologies in these days of international goodwill. Knowing the length of your vessel, you throw a piece of wood into the water, level with the bow, and count the number of seconds it takes to pass the stern!

If your vessel is 50 feet long and the time taken for the wood to pass the stern is 5 seconds the proportion would be: 50 : 5 : : 6,080 : the number of seconds to cover one mile, in which case it is 600 seconds or 10 minutes. This means that you will do one mile in 10 minutes and so your speed is 6 knots.

Remember, a knot is not a distance, but a speed of 1 mile per hour.

For the Dutchman's log, all you need is a supply of bits of wood, unless you tie a line to one. How economical can you get?

CHAPTER FIVE

ACTUAL POSITION

Now that we have discovered how to measure speed and distance through the water by means of some kind of log, we can, as I said before, find where we should be at any given time by measuring the distance run along the course steered. Thus we get the D.R. position.

It is very seldom that our actual position coincides at any time with this D.R. position, and if we can find our actual position by some means, the difference between this fix and the D.R. position at the same time will give the set and drift of the current. The set is the direction of the current measured from the D.R. position towards the fix, and the drift is the distance between these two positions measured in miles.

If this drift was, say, four miles in two hours, then the rate of the current would be four divided by two, i.e. two knots. The diagram illustrates what I have just said.

Notice that, for this diagram, a log is being used which gives the distance run through the water, instead of the speed which we found with the two logs already described. This recording log can be set at zero at the beginning of the voyage and not touched until it is taken in when you get to your destination, just like the trip meter on a car speedometer.

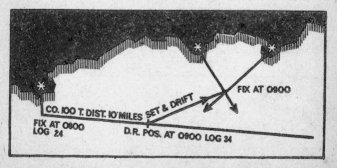

It consists of a small cylinder with fins on it, set in such a way that, when towed through the water, it rotates and turns the towing line. This line is fastened to a governor wheel which in turn is hooked on to a revolving spindle in the log clock.

This clock records the miles by the number of turns the rotator makes. The clock is fastened to the taffrail aft, or to a boom amidships.

Now work the following examples on the Dover Straits chart.

PROBLEM 1.

"A vessel left Folkestone Gp. Fl. Lt. at 0800 hrs. and steered 214°T at a speed of 4 knots. At 1000 hrs. Mydley Chapel bore 289°T and Dungeness High Lt. bore 256°T. Find (a) The D.R. position at 1000 hrs.
      (b) The position by cross bearings at 1000 hrs.
      (c) The set and drift of the current."

PROBLEM 2.

"A vessel left Folkestone Gp. Fl. Lt. at 2000 hrs. steering 069°T at a speed of 4 knots. At 2200 hrs. the flashing white light on Dover Breakwater bore 316°T and South Foreland Lt. bore 007°T.
Find (a) The D.R. position at 2200 hrs.
      (b) The fix by cross bearings at 2200 hrs.
      (c) The set and drift of the current"
Answers will be found on page 157.

In the first of the above questions it was easy enough for me to say that we took a bearing of Mydley Chapel. In actual practice it would be very difficult to pick out Mydley Chapel with any certainty, from among all the rest of the churches you see scattered about Romney Marsh. It is very important that you should pick the right church, for laying off the bearings from the wrong point of reference may lead you into trouble.

To check these points, the thing to do is to get a fix using two points of whose identity you are certain. At the same time, take bearings of other points which may be useful later. By laying the bearings of these off on the chart from the fix, they may be identified.

If you frequent the same part of the coast most of the time, you can by this means get to know it like the back of your hand, and there may come a time when such knowledge is vital to you. The least little thing can be important.

In one part of the world where fog is very prevalent they are said to have what are called "dog-barking" sailors. When sailing along their coasts in fog, they can tell their position by the barking of the dogs kept by people on different farms, just by the tone and pitch of the bark. This may or may not be true, but it illustrates my point, and it's a good story anyway.

I wonder if, when a farmer gets a new dog, they bring out a Notice to Mariners about it. Locally, of course.

Our questions asked for the set and drift of the current. This was not strictly accurate, as a current is a movement of water which is always in the same direction, for instance the Thames or any other river in its upper reaches, or the Gulf Stream. The symbol on the chart for this is ⋙⟶ or ∿∿∿∿∿⟶

The movement of water round our coasts however, is tidal, and varies from hour to hour as the tide ebbs and flows. The symbol for the flood tide is ⫫⟶ and for the ebb ⟶

Tidal information is given in the South East corner of our chart in the shape of tables giving the direction and rate of the tide for every hour of the tide at Dover, for spring and neap tides, for different locations on the chart bearing symbols thus: ◈ This one appears near the first course we took from Folkestone and, knowing the time of High Water at Dover, we could find the direction and rate of the tide to expect during our passage.

Please do not hold it against me that the set of the tide in this question does not appear in the appropriate table. Do not let this undermine your confidence, as the question is quite hypothetical.

The tide arrows are only used when there is insufficient information available for the construction of tables.

CHAPTER SIX

COUNTERACTING CURRENTS

The purpose in finding the set and drift of the tide or current at any time is that, assuming we will continue to be set in the same direction at the same rate for some time, we can take steps to counteract such a deviation from the course we want to make good. We must make an alteration of course which will offset the effect of the current exactly.

Most of my readers are used to thinking for themselves. Some are well versed in the various sciences, including physics, and a few, as soon as this proposition is stated, will know how it should be done.

I want to ask something very difficult from all of you. I want you to put away all your ideas on the subject, to put your hand in mine and follow a few very simple instructions.

The method I shall outline is the correct one. There may be other correct methods. I doubt it. What I do know is that there are several methods which are definitely wrong, and which have a great fascination for the embryo navigator. I won't describe them, you can easily find them for yourself, but why take the trouble?

When making your way from one place to another place, by a known course through a current whose direction and strength we know, our problem is to find the course to steer. Here is an example:

How it is done:

Find the course to steer to make good a course of 070 T. when steaming at 8 knots through a tidal stream setting 310 T. at 2 knots.

Lay off the course to be made good, AB. From A lay off the direction of the tidal stream AC, and mark off along it 2 miles from A to D. This is the set and drift for one hour. (On a chart the Latitude scale would be used for miles, of course.)

With centre D and a radius on the compasses equal to the

distance steamed in the same interval (i.e. 8 miles, since the interval is one hour), cut the line AB at E. DE is the course to steer from A to make good the course AB.

At the same time AE is the distance made good towards B on one hour and is therefore the speed made good. This is the correct and only way to solve this problem; a very provocative statement, though not intended as such.

I once made up a jingle about this and somebody else thought it good enough to take it away with them, so here it is from memory.

> "To make a course from A to B
> Lay off the set from A to C
> The rate along AC to D
> From D the vessel's speed to E
> DE is now the course to steer,
> The speed made good, AE, is clear."

This is not poetry, for it is intelligible at once, and does not conjure up visions which are not contained in the actual words. Let's just call it a mnemonic.

It is also possible from this figure to work out the time it will take under the same conditions to get to one's destination. If, in the diagram, A is the starting point and B is the destination, then the time taken, which is equal to distance divided by speed, is equal to the length of AB divided by the length of AE.

It often happens that AE is a very awkward number consisting of something in the nature of 7.35. To avoid having to divide by such a number, draw a line through B parallel

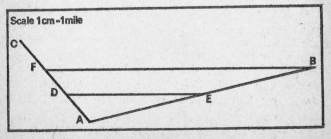

Scale 1cm – 1mile

29

to DE to cut the line AC at F. It so happens that $\frac{FB}{DE}=\frac{AB}{AF}$, so all you have to do is to divide FB by the given ship's speed, in this case 8 knots, and this is a much simpler operation.

Here are a couple of exercises for you to try.

PROBLEM 1.

Find the course to steer from a position one mile 270°T. from C. d'Alprech Lt. Ho., to a position 3 miles 270°T. from Paris Plage Lt. Ho., to counteract the effect of a tidal stream setting 225°T. at 2 knots, ship steaming at 6 knots.

Find also the speed made good, and the time it will take to reach the destination.

PROBLEM 2.

From the position in Qu. 1 off Paris Plage Lt. Ho., find the course to steer to a position 3 miles 225°T. from Pt. de Haut Banc Lt. Ho. to counteract the effect of a tidal stream setting 315°T. at 1½ knots, ship steaming at 5 knots.

Find also the speed made good and the time taken to reach the destination.

I hope that the two paragraphs before the above questions are not too fearsome. It is in cases like this that the mind boggles at a stream of letters of the alphabet which are quite meaningless; except that they refer in this case to the diagram, and constant reference must be made to it.

Work systematically. Each time a line or point is referred to, find the line or point on the diagram, and I guarantee that even after one reading you will be well on the way to understanding this particular operation.

This is the secret, if it can be called a secret, of working from a written explanation, and it takes just a little application on the part of the learner.

In finding the course to steer to counteract a current, it happens that the wrong course is very little different from the correct one, within perhaps 1°, so when checking the answers at the end of the book, be guided more by the correctness of the speed made good and the time taken, as a mistake in the method will be more noticeable here.

CHAPTER SEVEN

ADJUSTING YOUR COURSE

Having learned from the last chapter how to set a course to counteract a current, we must take into consideration the fact that the current we get while on this course may vary from the one we expect, and so it is necessary to check on it from time to time.

This is done by getting a fix, and comparing it with the Dead Reckoning position obtained by plotting the course and distance steered up to the time of taking the fix. The direction from the D.R. position to the fix will be the actual set of the tide, and the distance between the two positions will be the actual drift.

An adjustment can then be made to the course for the new conditions.

EXAMPLE

In the figure below a vessel is steering a course DE from A to counteract a current setting AD, so that she will make a course AB. After a certain period she finds herself at position G. AF is the course steered and distance steamed in the time elapsed from A until the fix at G and, without any tide, she would be at position F. The actual set and drift is therefore FG.

PROBLEM 1.

Find the course to steer from the Royal Sovereign Lt. V. to Dungeness Lt. Ho. to counteract a current setting 080°T. at 2 knots, ship's speed 6 knots.

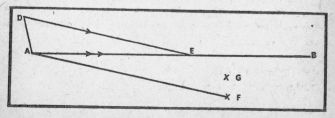

After steaming for two hours on this course, Dungeness Lt. Ho. bore 051°T. and Rye Church bore 329°T. Find the actual set and drift.

A Running Fix

For a cross bearing we use two points whose positions are known on the chart, three if possible – to make sure that we have selected in reality the points from which we lay off our bearings on the chart.

For while any two bearings will always cross at one point, three will only cross at one point on the chart if they are taken accurately and the correct points observed.

If you have selected a wrong mark on the shore in conjunction with two others, your mistake will appear immediately you lay off the bearings.

While it is very convenient to be able to fix the position by cross bearings it is not always possible, and we are obliged to investigate other means of doing this. Very often there is only one lighthouse or mark available on which to check our progress, and in this case we can get what is called a "running fix" by taking two bearings of the object with an interval between them.

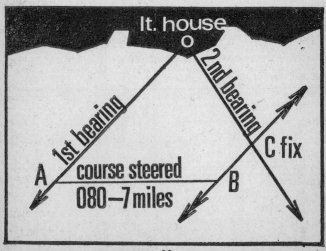

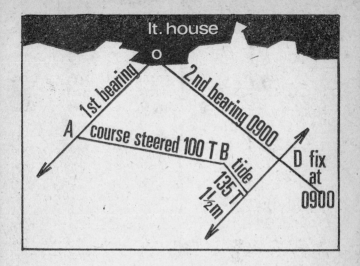

A vessel steaming at 080°T at 7 knots sees a lighthouse bearing 039°T, and 1 hour later the same lighthouse bears 325°T. Find the position of the ship at the time of taking the second bearing.

Lay off the two bearings through the position of the lighthouse.

From any point A on the first bearing lay off the course and measure 7 miles along it to B. Through B draw a line parallel to the first bearing to cut the second bearing at C, which is the required position.

PROBLEM 2.

A vessel steering 045°T at 8 knots sees Dungeness Lt. Ho. bearing 000°T and 45 mins. later it bore 300°T.

Find the position of the ship at the time of taking the second bearing.

When, during the run between the two bearings, the ship is affected by a known tidal stream this can be allowed for as follows:

At 0800 a vessel steaming 100°T at 7 knots sees a lighthouse bearing 040°T and at 0900 it bore 305°T. During this time the tide was estimated to be setting 135°T at a rate of

1½ knots. Find the ship's position at 0900.

Lay off the two bearings as before. From any point A on the first bearing lay off the course for 7 miles to B, and from B lay off the tide for 1½ miles to C. Draw a line through C parallel to the first bearing to cut the second bearing at D, which will be the position required at 0900.

PROBLEM 3.

At 1200 a vessel steaming 225°T at 6 knots observed C. Gris Nez Lt. Ho. to bear 180°T and at 1300 it bore 090°T. The tide was estimated to be setting 025°T at 2 knots.

Find the ship's position at 1300.

PROBLEM 4.

At 1800 a vessel steaming 270°T at 8 knots observed the Royal Soveriegn Lt. V. to bear 320°T and at 1900 it bore 040°T. The tide was estimated to be setting 080°T at 2 knots. Find the bearing and distance of the ship from the Lt. Vessel at 1900.

CHAPTER EIGHT

RULES OF THE ROAD

While we have been sailing up and down the Straits of Dover in theory, with a fine disregard for anything other than trying to get to where we want to go, it is as well to remember that the seas are free, and that there are many others such as we afloat. And indeed, some with a great deal more right to be there, in that they are working while we are enjoying ourselves.

In fact, there are so many craft about that there is often danger of them bumping into each other, and a whole system of lights, signals and manoeuvres has been devised for preventing such unfortunate occurrences.

The importance of this system cannot be over-emphasised, and it is published by the Stationery Office in pamphlet form as "Regulations for preventing collisions at Sea."

There are 31 rules to this end, and a thorough knowledge of these is essential. At one time candidates for Board of Trade Certificates were required to repeat them word for word, so important are they, and it still delights the examiners to find candidates who can perform this feat. They are compiled internationally, and in September 1965 an amended set of rules came into force. So if you buy them, be sure to get the latest.

To understand the rules it is necessary to have some idea of the anatomy of a ship. For instance the sharp end is the bow and the blunt end is the stern, with apologies for such an insult to your intelligence.

The fore and aft line is a line joining the bow to the stern, and the beam is at right angles to the fore and aft line amidships.

The right hand side of the ship when facing forward is the starboard side, and the other side is the port side.

An object is on your starboard bow when it bears between the bow and the starboard beam, and it is before the beam.

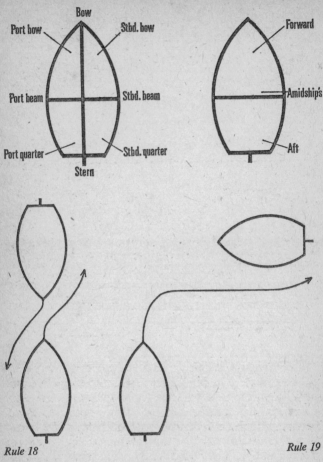

Rule 18

Rule 19

Similarly with an object bearing on the port side, port bow, before the port beam.

When it bears between the starboard beam and the stern it is then abaft the beam and on the starboard quarter.

When it bears between the port beam and the stern, it is then abaft the beam on the port quarter.

The fore or forward part of the ship is in front, and the after part behind the middle, which is amidships.

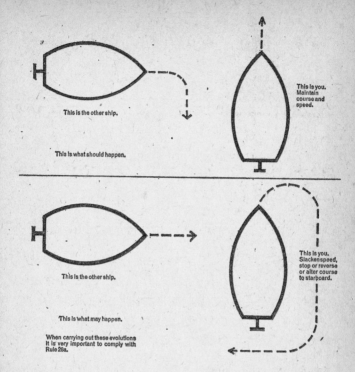

This is the other ship.

This is what should happen.

This is you. Maintain course and speed.

This is the other ship.

This is what may happen.

When carrying out these evolutions it is very important to comply with Rule 28a.

This is you. Slacken speed, stop or reverse or alter course to starboard.

There are many definitions in the Rules and it is important to know them. A power driven vessel, for example is one propelled by machinery whether under sail or not, and there is a special day signal to be carried by a vessel under sail and power at the same time (Rule 14). The rule of the road for power driven craft says that when two such vessels are meeting end on, they both alter course to starboard (to the right) so that each passes on the port side of the other (Rule 18).

In narrow waters one should keep to that side of the channel which lies on one's starboard side, in other words you keep to the right, as opposed to keeping to the left on our roads (Rule 25).

When power-driven craft are crossing and where there

is risk of collision, the craft with the other on her own starboard side keeps out of the way of the other, that is, you keep out of the way of the vessel on your right (Rule 19). At night you would see her red side-light, red for danger (Rule 2).

She would see your green side-light, (Rule 2) and would maintain her course and speed (Rule 21).

It will be found, on a close perusal of the Rules for Preventing Collisions at Sea, that when you are in power-driven vessel and risk of collision exists with another vessel, it will probably be your duty to keep clear of her. It is your duty to maintain your course and speed only when the danger comes from another power-driven vessel or the equivalent (a vessel towing, for instance) crossing from your port bow (Rule 19), or from any vessel overtaking you (Rule 24).

Maintaining your course and speed can be nerve-racking if the other vessel does not show any sign of keeping out of your way. In such a case, with a power-driven vessel crossing from your port bow, you should give five short and rapid blasts on the whistle. (Rule 28b). This is to call his attention to your dissatisfaction with the state of affairs, and where a whistle is not available some other means should be used.

A collision must be avoided at all costs, however, and, if he doesn't take avoiding action, you must, by slackening speed, stopping, or reversing, or by altering course to starboard and taking a round turn out of her if necessary. In this case you should not alter to port to go round the other vessel's stern.

It may be that when you meet other vessels you are proceeding under sail only. In that case, power-driven vessels must keep out of your way whenever risk of collision exists between you and them. There is a short Rule however, numbered 29, on which you must keep your weather eye. If, for instance, you are tacking from one side of the fairway to the other going up the Thames, and a passenger liner is coming down, it seems a bit hard to expect her, drawing over thirty feet, to keep clear of you drawing thirty inches.

I would consider this a special circumstance and make discretion the better part of valour, a cliché which means in this case that you should not get in her way.

In the open sea things would be different. She would then be able to keep out of your way, but always keep in mind that when there is a great disparity in size, you are going to get the worst of a collision, so don't stick your neck out.

The Rules should be obeyed however, and where there is room for all to manoeuvre the ordinary practice of them should be carried out.

Let us suppose that you yourself are in a vessel under sail only and that you are in yacht-infested waters. The Rule governing the behaviour of sailing vessels when risk of collision exists between them is No. 17. Before actually dealing with the Rule we must get a few more nautical terms straight.

The tack of a sail is the lower forward corner. In most sailing craft this is made fast either to the bow or to the foot of the mast, but in the days of square rigged ships it was made fast on the windward side of the ship. This meant that when the wind was on the port side, the tack was made fast to the port side, and the ship was said to be on the port tack. When the wind was on the starboard side the ship was on the starboard tack because the tack was made fast to the starboard side.

So it is to this day, except that the tack remains fast in the centre line. When the wind is on your port side you are on the port tack, when the wind is on your starboard side you are on the starboard tack.

If you want to sail North, and the wind is North, you will find that you can't. It is necessary to steer some way from North so that the sails will fill, but also to sail as close to the wind as possible. To do this you haul the sheets aft as close as possible and bring the boat round into the wind until the luff begins to shake, the luff being the forward edge of the sail. You are then "close-hauled", sailing as near the wind as possible.

As soon as you leave the close-hauled position by bringing the wind further aft you are "running free". You can therefore be close-hauled or free to port, or close-hauled or free to starboard.

A NEW SIMPLICITY

In September, 1965, this Rule assumed a simplicity which is the work of genius and it says when there is a risk of collision between two sailing vessels, one of them shall keep out of the way of the other as follows:

(a) When they have the wind on different sides the vessel with the wind on the port side shall keep out of the way of the other.

(b) When they have the wind on the same side the vessel

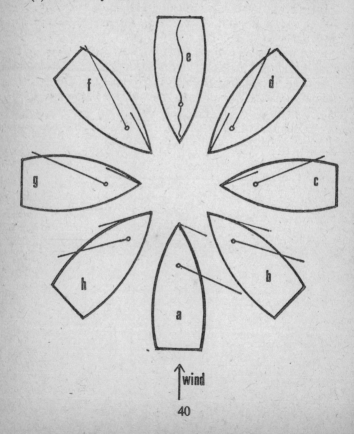

↑wind

40

to windward keeps out of the way of the vessel to leeward.

The windward side is that side opposite the side on which the mainsail is carried. This is easy to understand, except perhaps when the wind is right aft. Then, if the mainsail is out to starboard, the port side is the windward side, and if the mainsail is out on the port side, the starboard side is the windward side. I have not quoted the Rule verbatim, by the way.

The Rule of the Road for sailing vessels can be illustrated as follows:

If we consider that we are in vessel A then for each other vessel we keep out of the way.

If we consider ourselves in vessel H then we keep out of the way of E, F, and G, but maintain our course and speed for A, B, C, and D.

In G we keep out of the way of F and E but stand on for the rest, and so on.

Vessel E is going about from one tack to the other and should be watched carefully to see which tack she pays off on.

CHAPTER NINE

EFFECT OF TIDE

I should imagine that it is fairly easy for anyone to arrive at the conclusion that, if you are steaming at 7 knots and the tide is setting with you at 2 knots, your effective speed will be 9 knots. And that, if it was setting against you, you would only be doing 5 knots.

This effective speed is also known as the "speed made good", while the speed steamed at is the speed through the water – the difference being due to the fact that the whole body of water is moving.

This is quite a difficult conception. I seem to remember a seafaring conundrum which posed a vessel steaming against a six knot current at eight knots when a man falls overboard and the question was, "At what speed would she have to steam the opposite way to catch up with him and effect his rescue?"

The answer of course was, "Any speed she liked," because, as soon as she stopped, the distance between her and the man could remain constant, since they are both stopped in the water even though they are both moving over the ground at the same speed, namely, the speed of the current. All she has to do is to steam back and pick him up.

Currents are blamed for a great deal at sea. They always seem to set stronger against you than with you, and you always use more fuel steaming against one than with one, even in the same time. Ask any Chief Engineer. Another funny thing is that the log seems to turn faster when you are steaming against the tide. Ah, you think I'm pulling your legs now? Quite right. Nevertheless, these notions all have some upholders.

Having made you think a bit, I hope, about tide, let us see its effect on the course and speed when it is setting in some other direction than directly against or directly with us.

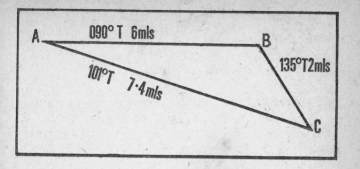

Consider a vessel steaming 090°T at 6 knots in a current setting 135°T at 2 knots.

She starts her run at A, and at the end of the first hour she should be at B, but in the meantime the water surrounding her has moved and in effect she has also been moving in a direction and for a distance equal to BC. At the end of one hour, then, she will be at C and has gone from A to C. Therefore AC is the course made good and the distance AC is the effective speed or speed made good. So long as conditions remain the same, she will continue to make this course and speed good.

Let us combine this with a running fix, the problem we did in Chapter 7.

A vessel sees point A bearing 045°T and after steaming for 4 miles on a 098°T course through a current which set her 330°T for one mile the same point bore 335°T. Find her position at the time of taking the second bearing, and if she continues on this course find the distance she will be off point B when it is abeam.

From the diagram, the vessel steams from any point X on the first bearing for 4 miles to Y and is set 1 mile to Z. Transfer the first bearing through Z to cut the second bearing at C, which is the position required on that bearing.

XZ is the course being made good, and if we continue this course from C she will be abeam of point B at position D. Notice that the beam bearing, being a bearing relative to the ship's head direction, is at 90° to XY. Notice also that if

43

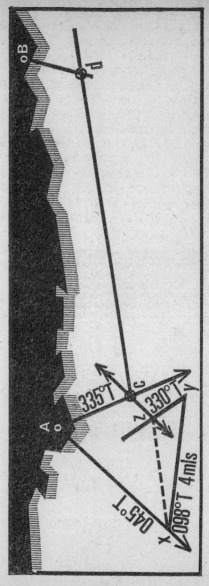

oB

D

A o

335°T

C

330°T

z

y

045°T

x

098°T 4 mls

860

44

the line CD is produced backwards it will cut the first bearing at the point where the vessel actually was when she was on that bearing. This is not important.

Here are two examples for you to work out.

(1) A vessel steering a course of 060°T at 6 knots sees Beachy Head Lt. H. bearing 012°T at 0800, and forty minutes later it bore 322°T. During this time the tide was estimated to be setting 077°T for a distance of one mile. Find the position at 0840. If she continues on this course how far will she pass off the Royal Sovereign Lt. V. when it is abeam?

(2) At 1600 a vessel steering 235°T at 5 knots sees the South Foreland Lt. Ho. bearing 290°T, and one hour later it bore 010°T, current estimated at 200°T, 1 knot. Find the ship's position at 1700. If she continues on this course, find her distance off Dungeness Lt. Ho. when it is abeam.

CHAPTER TEN

LET'S GO TO FRANCE

Now is a good time to look back and see just how much of the chartwork we have covered. We have plotted positions on the chart and taken positions from the chart; we can fix our position by cross bearings or by a running fix, lay off a course from one place to another, making allowance for a tide, and we can set a course to counteract a tide.

We can find the distance between two places, and the time it will take us to get there at a certain speed. In fact, except for one thing, we are now ready to set out on a voyage. Since this is not a voyage in fact, we will ignore this one thing and go. Later we will include it and go again.

We will go from Folkestone to Treport in France, a port you will find at the bottom edge of the chart. We are going in a craft drawing less than six feet of water and capable of cruising at five knots.

(1) Lay off the Courses as follows:
From Folkestone Lt. Ho. to the Varne Buoy, thence to the B.W. Buoy off the north end of the Bassure de Baas, continuing on this course to 1 mile past the buoy, thence to a position just West of the R.W. Buoy off the entrance to the R. Canche, and thence direct to Treport breakwater. Find the direction and distance on each course, and the time taken between each alteration of course if the speed is 5 knots.

(2) It is expected that for the first 2 hours the tide will be setting 049°T at 1 knot. Find the course to steer to counteract this tide, vessel's speed 5 knots. Find also the time of arrival at the Varne Buoy if she left Folkestone Lt. Ho. at 0800 hrs.

(3) From the Varne Buoy it is expected that the tide will set 030°T at 2 knots. Find the course to steer to get to the next buoy steaming at 5 knots, and find the effective speed towards that destination.

(4) At 1130 C. Gris Nez Lt. Ho. bore 113°T, and half an hour later it bore 076°T, vessel now steering 165°T between

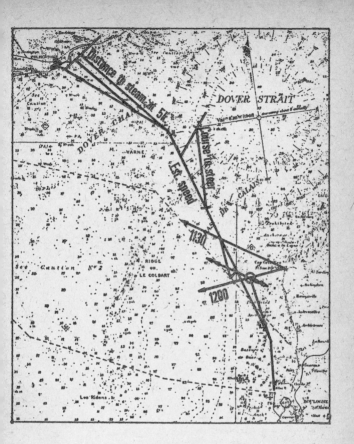

the two bearings and the tide estimated to be setting 030°T at one knot, vessel's speed 5 knots. Find her position at 1200.

(5) Having got so far safely, let us not push our luck too far. Pick up the B.W. buoy and then make for Boulogne.

ON TO TREPORT

(6) Outside Boulogne Harbour the vessel resumes her course towards the R.W. buoy off the mouth of the R. Canche. At 0800 C. d'Alprech Lt. Ho. bore 165°T, and at 0830

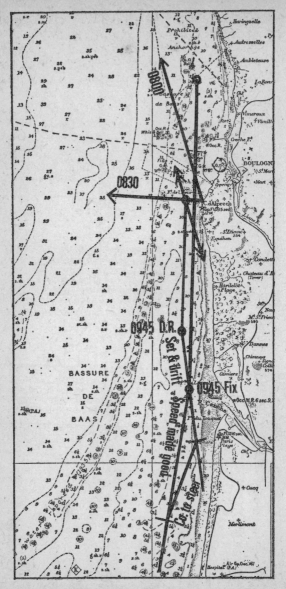

0800

0830

0945 D.R.

0945 Fix

Set & drift

Speed made good

Co. to steer

BOULOGN

BASSURE
DE
BAAS

it was abeam. Bearing 094°T, vessel steaming at 5 knots in slack water. Find her distance off the Lt. Ho. at 0830.

(7) At 0945 the vessel found herself at the R.W. buoy, having steamed on the same course at 5 knots. Find the set and rate of the current and find the True course to steer from the buoy to Treport Breakwater to counteract this current.

(8) At 1045, steaming at 5 knots Paris Plage Lt. Ho. bore 028°T and Pt. de Haut Banc Lt. Ho. bore 146°T. Find the actual set and drift of the tide and reset the course to Treport, reducing speed to 4 knots because of the shortage of fuel. Find also the estimated time of arrival at Treport.

Let us suppose that the rest of the trip is uneventful and that we arrive at Treport at 1500, having on our way gone through most of the processes we learnt in previous exercises.

CHAPTER ELEVEN

VARIATION & DEVIATION

Until now all our courses and bearings have been given as True, and this makes navigation very much simpler, but the only way to get True bearings from a compass is to see that it is a gyro compass. This will be outside the means of most yachtsmen, I expect, and we must make do with a magnetic compass.

This is not such a hardship, as navigators have been finding their way about by this means ever since it was found that if a magnetic needle was suspended freely on the surface of the earth, it always came to rest pointing in the same direction. With the advance of knowledge in physical science, this attractive power was recognized as a magnetic field covering the earth, and caused by what seemed to be a large magnet inside the earth with one end in the north of Canada. This attracts the compass north point.

The exact cause of this magnetic effect is not known, but the magnetic pole is moving gradually eastward, so it must have a fluid cause of some kind. It is as though the earth were a solenoid with electrons flowing round it from East to West, giving a magnetic pole North and South. How this comes about is anybody's guess, and the field for discovery here is wide open.

As far as we are concerned, it is a great pity that the Magnetic North Pole does not coincide with the True North Pole for this fact causes what is called Variation. Variation is the angle between the true and magnetic meridians at any place and has a value ranging from 0° to 180°. If you were between the two Poles the Variation would be 180°, and if you were somewhere where the two poles were in line with you, the Variation would be nil.

Variation is really the angle between the True and Magnetic Poles, for practical purposes. It is named West when the Magnetic Pole is to the left of the True Pole, and East when to the right of the True Pole. In the Straits of Dover the

Variation is at present about 6¼°W. In fifty years it will be nil.

The magnetic compass points to the Magnetic North, which means that off Dover it will be 6° out, its N. point will be pointing 6° to the West of True North, so that 000°T is the same direction as 006°M. From this we can deduce that, given a True course or bearing, we must add a Westerly Variation to get the Magnetic course or bearing.

To get a True course or bearing from a Magnetic course or bearing, we must subtract a Westerly Variation. A very common aid to memory when converting True to Magnetic or vice versa is the rule "Variation West, Magnetic Best." i.e.,

Course	162°T	
Variation	6°W	
Course	168°M	

Of the two courses, T and M, M is best (greater). When comparing only two things, the word should be "better." I know this, but "better" won't rhyme with "West."

When you have laid off the course on the chart and found its True direction, you must apply the Variation to it before you can steer the course by the magnetic compass. You must be able to do this by the above rule. At the same time, there is nothing to stop you taking the course from the magnetic compass rose on the chart instead of from the true rose or the meridian. If it is an old chart you may be a couple of degrees out, but by this method you will never apply the Variation the wrong way.

Some charts do not have magnetic roses on them, and the Variation is given by lines passing through places having the same Variation.

These lines are called isogonic lines. Using such a chart, you would have to apply the Variation to the courses as above. Try one or two examples.

Using Variation 6°W, convert the following True courses to Magnetic. 072°T 106°T 159°T 202°T 268°T 315°T 356°T.

Using Variation 6°W, convert the following Magnetic bearings to True. 004°M 117°M 148°M 216°M 292°M 327°M 357° M.

DEVIATION

Do you remember at school how we magnetized our pen knives by stroking the blade with a magnet? The blade became magnetized not by the touch of the magnet but by the magnetic field round the magnet.

In the same way the earth's magnetic field magnetizes all the iron and steel on the earth, and these metals in the shape of the objects they form, take on magnetism whose polarity depends on the direction in which each object is lying.

In the case of a wooden boat this effect does not apply, but in a metal boat, or in one with metal fittings or an engine, some magnetism will be acquired, and this will affect the compass. A further misfortune is that the effect of this magnetism changes on going from one course to another, because with change of direction, the boat's polarity takes on a different aspect to the compass needle.

The boat's polarity causes what is called Deviation, and this must be applied to magnetic courses to bring them to compass courses or vice versa, and to compass bearings to bring them to magnetic bearings.

It is usual to combine the Variation and Deviation into what is called the Compass Error, by adding them together algebraically, i.e., same names add, or, if they are of opposite names, subtract and name the same as the larger.

The Deviation is named West when the Compass North is to the left of Magnetic North and East when the Compass North is to the right of Magnetic North.

Given a Variation of 6°W the following Deviation would give the Compass Errors shown:

Variation	6°W	6°W	6°W
Deviation	5°W	5°E	7°E
Compass Error	11°W	1°W	1°E

Using the same Variation find the error of the compass when the Deviation is: 10°W- 9°E 2°W 0°. 1°E 6°E.

52

When applying the Deviation or the Compass Error, the rule is much the same as the one we had for applying the Variation.

Deviation or Compass Error West, Compass Best.

Deviation or Compass Error East, Compass Least.

Now you.

	006°M		084°M			272°M		316°M
Dev.	4°W		7°E	Dev.		6°W		3°E
	010°C		077°C					

	069°C		142°C			187°C		216°C
Dev.	2°E		10°W	Dev.		8°E		5°W
	071°M		132°M					

In case it should be said that we are rule of thumb sailors, let me give you a theoretical figure which proves that the above rules are correct.

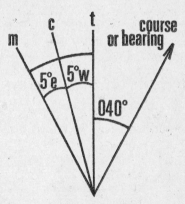

If the course or bearing is 040°T, the Variation 10°W, and the Deviation 5°E then from the figure it can be seen that the magnetic course or Bearing is 050° and the Compass course or bearing is 045°. T, M, and C are the True, Magnetic, and Compass Norths respectively.

Notice:
```
        050°M
Dev.     5°E
        ─────
        045°C (Compass least)
        ─────
```

In the above case the Compass Error is 5°W.
```
        040°T
Error    5°W
        ─────
        045°C (Compass Best)
        ─────
```

Some people use the diagram for applying errors, variations and deviations and it is a very good method. The method is always the same though the rules may differ, but the important thing is to get the correct answer or you will be a long way out of your reckoning.

To find the Compass error we can take a compass bearing of the Sun, the Moon, a star or a planet, work out the True bearing of the one we choose at the time, and compare the True bearing with the Compass bearing, for the difference between them is the Compass error.

I am just telling you this to frighten you because we are not going to do any such thing. We can generally find the Compass error by other and much simpler means.

For our purposes the Pole star always bears North so that if we get a bearing of it by the compass and assume that the True bearing is 000° we will not be more than 1° out in the Compass error because Polaris is within 1° of the Celestial pole. In case some of my readers cannot recognize the Pole star, here is how to find it.

The two end stars of the Plough or Great Bear point to it.

A much simpler method is to select two objects marked on the chart, find the True bearing of them when they are in transit, i.e., in line with each other, taken from the chart by the parallel rulers, then get a compass bearing of them when they are in line or in transit and compare the two bearings. The difference between the bearings will be the compass error.

*

to Polaris ↑

*
*   *
*   *
Plough   *
              *

Here are some examples.

Pole star bearing	000°T	
	010°C	Compass Best Error West
Error	10°W	

	360°T	
	350°C	Compass Least Error East
Error	10°E	

Two objects in line bearing	063°T	134°T
	074°C	122°C
Error	11°W	12°E

The purpose of finding the Compass error is to apply it to the True course to find the course to steer by the compass. It must also be applied to all bearings taken by the compass, so that they may be laid off on the chart.

Most important of all is to remember that there will be an alteration in the error for every alteration of course, because the amount of the deviation depends on the direction of the ship's head.

CHAPTER TWELVE

ANOTHER VOYAGE

Now that we know all about variation, deviation, and compass errors, it seems to me that the time is propitious for us to embark on another voyage.

We are certainly getting our 5p worth out of the chart we are using, and indeed, it may be a bit worn by this time. But if you want to renew it, remember that Nautical Booksellers are in business, that they are not charitable organizations, so send enough money to cover postage and packing at the very least.

The following questions are more difficult than those we did before, though they are of the same nature. I have given detailed working for them, and the answers. You may follow the working step by step, or do the questions first and look at the answers afterwards.

DOVER STRAIT CHART
No. 5116
Variation 6W. No deviation.

(1) Find the compass courses and the distance on each course from the South Sand Head Lt. V. to the F.G. Lt. at Eastbourne, passing Dungeness Lt. at a distance of 1 m., altering course when abeam of it to a position 1 m. 180°T from the Royal Sovereign Lt. V., thence to the destination.

Method:—With centre Dungeness Lt. Ho. and radius 1 m. or 1 minute of Latitude (which is the same thing) draw an arc of a circle to seaward of the Lt. Ho.

Lay off the bearing 180°T from the Royal Sovereign and measure 1 m. along it for the second alter course position, remembering that the position of a Lt. V. is at the centre of its keel.

Now draw the course line from the South Sand Head Lt. V. to touch the arc drawn off Dungeness, and a line through the Lt. at right angles to this course will give the position at which to alter course.

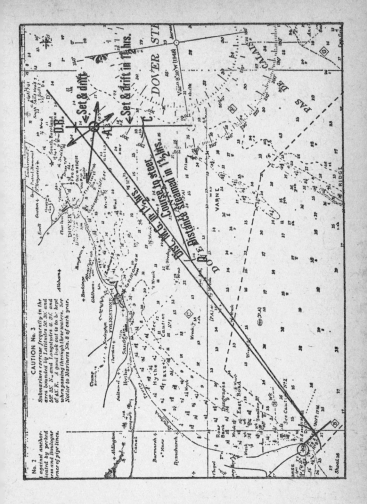

Join this position to the position South of the Royal Sovereign, and then this latter position to the F.G. Lt. at Eastbourne.

We now have three different courses and we can therefore get the answers to the question by taking each True course from the chart and converting it to Magnetic or Compass, which in this particular case are the same since there is no deviation.

Sand Head Lt. V. to Dungeness

	Course	230°T
	Variation	6°W

Course   236°M

Distance 23 miles

Measure the distance by taking 10 m. on the dividers, put one end on the Light Vessel and step along the course, altering the dividers for the last little bit. Two steps is twenty miles, and the little bit is three miles.

Dungeness to the Royal Sovereign

	Course	239°T
	Variation	6°W

Course   245°M

Distance 23.8 miles

Royal Sovereign to Eastbourne

	Course	306°T
	Variation	6°W

Course   312°M

Distance 7.2 miles

(2) Soon after leaving S. Sand Head Lt. V., a transit bearing of South Foreland Lt. Ho. in line with Ewell Church bore 283° by compass. Find the deviation for the direction of the ships head and the revised compass course, using the compass error found from the transit bearing.

Method:—One of the most certain and easy ways of finding the compass error is by transit bearing. First be certain that the two points are positively identified by you and that they are marked on the chart. Take a compass bearing of them when they come into line, and then lay one edge of the parallel rulers through the two points on the chart and find out what the True bearing is.

In this case the

transit bearing is	279°T
It is also	283°C

∴ the Compass Error is   4°W (Compass Best)

The amended course

will therefore be	230°T
Compass Error	4°W
Course	234°C

I would advise you to find the deviation thus:—

True bearing	279°
Variation	6°W
Mag. Bearing	285°
Comp. Bearing	283°
Deviation	2°E (Compass Least)

As long as you are on this particular course, the deviation – and hence the compass error – will be the same. And indeed, for this direction of the ship's head, the deviation will always be 2°E providing you keep the larger steel objects on the vessel in the same place and that you do not put anything steel too close to the compass.

It follows, therefore, that if you have a deviation tabulated for the ship's head on every point of the compass, you will have a deviation card from which you can get the deviation for any course you want. I will be going into this in more detail later.

(3) Half an hour after leaving the South Sand Head Lt. V., vessel steaming at 5 knots, South Foreland Lt. bore 330°C and the Fl. Lt. on Dover Harbour West Breakwater bore 281°C. Using the error found from the transit bearing, find the ship's position and the set and drift of the current.

Method:—Measure 2½ miles along the course line from the Lt. V. for half an hour's run. This will give the D.R.

position. Then correct the bearings to bring them to True and lay them off on the chart.

S. Foreland	330°C
C. Error	4°W
Bearing	326°T
Breakwater Light	281°C
C. Error	4°W
Bearing	277°T

Where the two bearings cross is the ship's actual position. Lat. 51°06'.4 N. Long. 1°24'.7 E.

The set and drift of the current is from the D.R. position to the fix by cross bearings, i.e. 179°T, 0.9 miles.

(4) Reset the course by compass to the position off Dungeness, making allowance for the current found in Qu. 3 and allowing 5° for leeway due to a N.W. wind. Ship's speed 5 K. Variation 6°W. Deviation 2°E.

Find also the distance made good towards Dungeness in 3 hours.

Method:—Redraw the course line from the Fix to Dungeness.

Extend the set to the southward for a distance of 1½ hours rate, i.e. 0.9 × 3 = 2.7 miles from the fix to point C.

From C measure with the dividers the distance run in 1½ hours back on to the line, i.e., 7½ miles from C to D. This direction CD is the true course to steer to counteract the current and the distance AD is the distance made good towards Dungeness in 1½ hours. Double this for one part of the answer. 17.6 miles.

Course	249°T
Leeway (allowed into the wind)	5°
	254°T
Variation	6°W
	260°M
Deviation	2°E
Course to steer	258°C

Leeway is always applied to the True Course. It is caused by pressure of the wind on the ship's side, blowing her bodily to leeward, and is measured by the angle between the ship's fore and aft line and the track through the water.

To find out how much leeway you are making look aft and estimate this angle. It takes a lot of experience. When estimated it is allowed towards the wind as shown above.

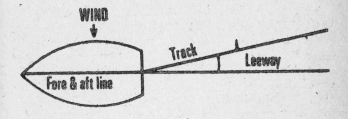

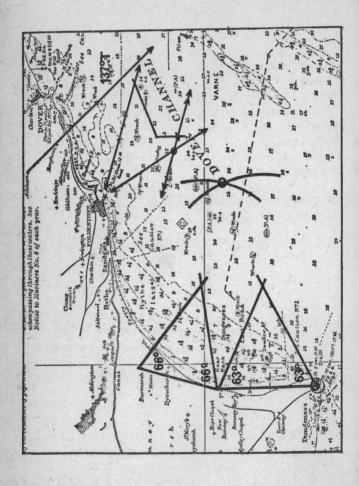

CHAPTER THIRTEEN

THE VOYAGE CONTINUED

(1) Continuing the voyage, Hougham and Alkham Churches in transit bore 325°C and shortly afterwards Folkestone
Lt. bore 295°C. After running for half an hour at 5 knots on
a course of 255°C with a current estimated to be setting
180°T at 2 knots. Folkestone Lt. bore 337°C.

Find the compass error and the position of the ship on the
second bearing of Folkestone Lt.

Method:—

True bearing of churches in transit from the chart 317°T.

		Folkestone Lt.	
Compass bearing	325°C		
	——	1st bearing	2nd bearing
Compass error	8°W	295°C	337°C
	——	8°W	8°W
Course	255°C	287°T	329°T
Error	8°W	——	——
	——		
	247°T		

Lay off the first bearing of course of 247°T for 2½ miles
and from this latter point the current of 180°T for 1 mile.

Draw a line through the end of the current parallel to the
first bearing. Lay off the second bearing of 329°T, and where
this cuts the transferred bearing, will be the required position
of the ship.

Lat. 51°1.3′N, 1°14.9′E Long.

(2) In view of the proximity of two dangerous wrecks near
the course line if we continue on this course, an alteration
was made to 214°C using a compass error of 8°W.

Find the angle subtended by Dungeness and Folkestone
Lts., which will clear the nearest of these wrecks by at least a
mile.

Method: This angle is what is called a horizontal danger angle. Let me recall some geometry for you. "The angles subtended by any chord of a circle at its circumference are equal." In the figure all the angles shown are equal, subtended by the chord AB, at the circumference of the circle.

If one of these angles is measured and we assume A and B are two points of land, then, as we steam past them, if the angle between them is less than the measured angle, it means that we are outside the circle, but if it is greater than the measured angle, we are inside the circle.

Going back to the problem, if we fix a point 1 mile outside the wreck and from this point measure the angle between Dungeness and Folkestone Lts. on the chart, then so long as our observed angles remain smaller than this angle we will be outside the arc of the circle passing through the two lights and the position outside the wreck. In this case the danger angle would be 104°.

This angle may be observed by a sextant, but if a sextant is not available, then the difference between the compass bearings of the lights would be sufficiently accurate.

Folkestone Lt. brg.	350°C
Dungeness Lt. brg.	248°C
	———
Angle subtended	102°

This angle would mean that we are outside the danger circle and are safe to proceed.

A very accurate fix may be obtained by the use of horizontal angles. It entails some geometric construction, but this is not outside the scope of anyone, and the results justify the means.

Let us assume that A and B are two points of land and that an observer at C sees the horizontal angle between the points to be 40°. This means that C can be anywhere on the circumference of a circle passing through A and B where the angle they subtend at the circumference is 40°. In the figure this state of affairs is illustrated.

The angle subtended by a chord of the centre of a circle is

exactly twice the angle at the circumference standing on the same chord, so that the subtended angle at 0, the centre of our circle, is twice the angle at C, 40°, and 0 will be 80°.

It is also true that the three angles in a triangle together make up 180°, so that in the triangle ABO, A and B are together equal to 100° and since AO and BO are equal, being radii of the same circle, angle A equals angle B equals 50°.

Note the relationship between the angles A and B and the angle C. A plus C = 90°, and for any angle C the angle at A will always be the difference between 90° and C.

I have brought you through the last few paragraphs to arrive at this conclusion, so you can now forget the process and hang on to the product.

When constructing a circle of position, therefore, from the horizontal angle subtended by two points of land, join them by a line and at each one erect an angle equal to the complement of the subtended angle, i.e., 90 minus the subtended angle. The two lines making these two angles will cross at the centre of the circle passing through the two points, and the ship's position. This is called a position circle. A combination of two of these circles will give a position fix at the point where they intersect. Let us put this into practice.

(3) With a compass the error of which was unknown the following Compass bearings were taken:—

Dungeness Lt.   252°
Tower near Romney   279°
Burmarsh Church   303°

Find the ship's position and the deviation of the compass for the direction of the ship's head if the variation is 6°W.

Method: First let us find the ship's position.

The horizontal angle between the tower and Dungeness from the above bearings is 279° minus 252°, which is 27°.

Draw a line between the light and the tower and at each end make an angle on the seaward side of 90° minus 27° = 63°.

With centre where the two lines cross and radius to the tower describe a circle.

The horizontal angle between the tower and the church from the above bearings is 24°.

Draw a line between the tower and the church and at each end make an angle of 66°.

With centre at the point where the two lines cross and radius to the tower, describe another circle.

The point at which the two circles intersect will be the ship's position. Of course they also intersect at the tower

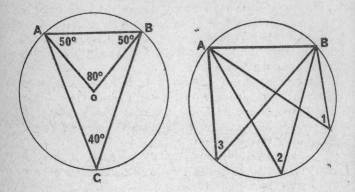

but it is to be hoped that the ship is at the other intersection. My answer to this part of the question is Lat. 50°58.8′N, Long. 1°12.6′E.

To find the compass error and the deviation, take the true bearing of any one of the three points from your position on the chart, and compare it with the compass bearing of the same point. For instance, Dungeness Lt. bears

	245°T
	252°C
Compass Error	7°W
Variation	6°W
Deviation	1°W

66

CHAPTER FOURTEEN

USING THE TIDE TABLES

When rounding Dungeness Point on the chart, it will be noticed that there is a letter enclosed in a diamond to the south-east. This refers to the tide tables at the bottom right hand corner of the chart.

Each small table has a letter at its head, and a position in Latitude and Longitude which is that of the same letter on the chart. The set of the tide is given for every hour of the tide at Dover as a Standard Time, and the rate is given for both Spring and Neap tides.

To use these tables it is necessary to have the times of H.W. at Dover, and also the range of the tide there. When this range is largest it is Spring tides, and when smallest it is Neap tides. Between these times some interpolation should be made for the rate of the tide.

If, for instance, we want to find the set and rate of the tide at position ⊕ at H.W. at Dover, on consulting the table at the foot of the chart we find that the tide is setting 031°T at a rate of 1.5K. at Springs and 0.8K. at Neaps. You musn't take this set and rate as being absolutely accurate, but it gives a very good indication of the tide you will experience at the stated time, and is the result of a series of observations at that place.

When going from, say Dungeness to Eastbourne, which is going to take some hours, you can allow for the tide you expect to get on an hourly basis, or, at once, for a period of several hours. The latter method is alright if you have plenty of sea room, while the former means more continuous work on the chart. But we will try an example of each.

Dover Strait Chart. Variation 6°W.

H.W. Dover 1200 Hours. Spring Tides

(1) At 1200 hrs. Dungeness Lt. Ho. bore 354°C and the tower S.W. of Lydd in transit with Gt. Cheyne Court bore 329°C, Ship's head 240°C. Find the ship's position and the deviation for the direction of the ship's head.

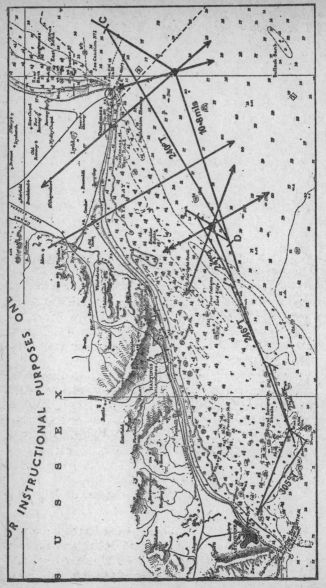

Method:—

From the chart transit bearing	=	321°T		321°T
	=	329°C	Var.	6°W
Compass Error		8°W		327°M
				329°C
			Dev.	2°W

Dungeness Lt. Ho. brg.	354°C
Comp. Error	8°W
Bearing	346°T

Posn. 50°50′.8 N. 1°00′ E.

(2) From this position set a course to pass just south of the red can buoy on the Royal Sovereign Shoals allowing for the tide given for position Ⓑ, and state the distance made good towards the destination in 3 hours, vessel's speed 5 K.

Method:—From the tide table it can be seen that at H.W. Dover the tide at Ⓑ is setting 031°T at a rate of 1.5K, in the next hour 031°T at 1.9K, and in the hour after that at 1.7K in an 031°T direction.

Since the question asks for the distance made good in a 3 hour period from the fix off Dungeness, lay off a line 031°T and measure 5.1 miles from the fix along this line to point C.

Now, with a radius of 15 miles on the dividers and centre C, cut the course line at D. CD is the required course and the distance from the fix to D is the distance made good in 3 hours. 5.1 miles is the drift due to tide in 3 hours, and 15 miles is the distance steamed in 3 hours.

Course to steer 239°T or 245°M, distance made good in 3 hrs. :—10.8 mls.

(3) At 1400 hours the Fl. R. Lt. at Rye Harbour entrance was in line with Iden Church bearing 342°C, and one hour later the Fl. R. Lt. at Hastings bore 301°C, tide setting 031°T at 1.5K, Course 249°C, ship's speed 5K. Find the position at

1500 hours and the deviation of the compass for the direction of the ship's head.

Method:

Transit Brg.	333°T			333°T
Compass Brg.	342°C		Var.	6°W
Compass Error	9°W			339°M
				342°C
			Dev.	3°W

Hastings Fl. R. Lt.	301°C
Compass Error	9°W
	292°T

Lay off the transit bearing and the bearing of the Hastings Lt. on the chart.

From anywhere on the transit bearing lay off the course of 240°T for 5 miles, and then from the end of the 5 miles lay off the tide 031°T for 1.5 miles. Through the end of the tide draw a line parallel to the transit bearing. Where this line cuts the bearing of the Hastings Lt. will be the position of the ship at 1500 hours.

Position 50°48.'6N, 0°45.'5E.

(4) From the position in the last question reset the course to pass just south of the red can buoy on the Royal Sovereign Shoal allowing for the Spring tide at position ⑱. Ship's speed 5K. Work out the course hour by hour and give the Estimated Time of Arrival (ETA) at the buoy.

Method:—1500 hours is 3 hours after H.W. Dover.
Tide is given as 031°T, 1.2K.

From the position lay off 031°T and measure along it 1.2 miles. From the end of the 1.2 miles as centre and radius 5 miles, cut the course line.

From the end of the current to this point is the course for the 1st hour.

Course 241°T, or 247°M.

For 4 hours after H.W. at Dover the tide is given as 031°T, 0.4K. From the position at the end of the 1st hour lay off 031°T for 0.4 miles and from the end of the 0.4 miles as centre and 5 miles radius, cut the course line.

From the end of the 0.4 miles to this point where the course line is cut will be the course to steer for the 2nd hour. Course 246°T or 252°M.

For 5 hours after H.W. at Dover the tide is given as 211°T, O.4K. From the position at the end of the 2nd hour lay off 211°T for 0.4 miles and from the end of the 0.4 miles as centre and radius 5 miles, cut the course line.

From the end of the 0.4 miles to this point where the course line is cut will be the course to steer for the 3rd hour. Course 252°T or 258°M.

Since we have only to steam about 4.2 miles to the buoy, and our effective speed is 5.2K, it will take us $\dfrac{4.2}{5.2} \times 60$ min. of the third hour to get there. This is equal to about $48\frac{1}{2}$ mins., so that we will arrive at our position south of the buoy at 1748 hours.

———————

(5) Having rounded the buoy at 1750 hours find the course to steer for the F. G. Lt. at Eastbourne to counteract the effect of the Spring tide at position Ⓑ, ship's speed 5K.

Method:—The time is now 6 hours after H.W. at Dover and the tide is given as setting 211°T at 1.3K.

From the position south of the Royal Sovereign buoy draw a direct course line to Eastbourne F.G. Lt. and at the beginning of this line the tide 211°T for 1.3 miles.

From the end of this tide as centre and with a radius of 5 miles, cut the course line.

From the end of the 1.3 miles to the point where the course line is cut will be the course to steer for this last leg. Course 305°T, or 311°M.

In actual practice, when steering in towards the land, the tide is much more easily counteracted by getting any two objects in transit and keeping them in line by heading up one way or the other. Always steer towards the nearer object to keep them on line. If it moves to the left steer to the left, if it moves to the right steer to the right. A little practice at this will enable you to get the right amount to steer off to keep them in line.

CHAPTER FIFTEEN

DEVIATION CARD

On a vessel which uses a magnetic compass it is necessary to construct a deviation card. This is a table of the deviations for directions of the ship's head right round the compass.

It is necessary to swing the vessel through 360° to enable bearings of a selected transit to be taken at angular intervals, but before doing this see that everything on board is in it's sea-going position, i.e., in the place where it will be when you are on a passage. See also that there is no iron near the compass in the shape of buckets, pans, knives, or even keys in your pocket.

Select a suitable transit on the shore as far away as possible and bring the ship slowly round. For every alteration of 20° in the direction of the ship's head take a bearing of the transit on the compass and make a note of it, then construct the table of deviations on the following page.

Do not think that this card is infallible, even when you take great care in making it up. All it will do is give you an approximate deviation with which to set the course, and some form of compass error should be obtained by means of a transit bearing or otherwise, as soon as possible after going on to a new course.

All sorts of things affect the deviation on the same heading: for instance, the engine may cause the deviation to vary when running, as opposed to being stopped, and if the vessel heels owing to wind pressure on the sails the deviation will definitely be different from when she is upright.

Don't be discouraged, however. Navigation is not an exact science, and you must make what allowance you can as accurately as you can; and when you come in sight of your destination, forget about the compass and steer for a known point.

Here is how to use the deviation card once it is made. Let us say that our course is 148°T, that the variation is 6°W and

Ship's Head Compass	Transit Brg. Compass	Transit Brg. Magnetic	Deviation	Ship's Head Magnetic
000	013	014	1 E	001
020	015	,,	1 W	019
040	018	,,	4 W	036
060	020	,,	6 W	054
080	022	,,	8 W	072
100	024	,,	10 W	090
120	021	,,	7 W	113
140	018	,,	4 W	136
160	014	,,	Nil	160
180	010	,,	4 E	184
200	008	,,	6 E	206
220	005	,,	9 E	229
240	006	,,	8 E	248
260	008	,,	6 E	266
280	011	,,	3 E	283
300	012	,,	2 E	302
320	013	,,	1 E	321
340	013	,,	1 E	341

that we want to know what course to steer by compass.

$$\begin{array}{ll}\text{Course} & 148°\text{T} \\ \text{Variation} & 6°\text{W} \\ \hline \text{Course} & 154°\text{M} \end{array}$$

On inspecting the column of magnetic headings, we find that 154°M is one quarter of the way between 160°M and 136°M; therefore the deviation will be one quarter of the difference between the deviation on 160°M and 136°M, which makes it 1°W. The compass course required is therefore

$$\begin{array}{ll}\text{Course} & 154°\text{M} \\ \text{Deviation} & 1°\text{W} \\ \hline \text{Course} & 155°\text{C} \end{array}$$

Since the deviation of the compass depends on the direction of the ship's head, as long as the ship is on this heading the deviation to be used for correcting compass bearings will be 1°W, and the compass error 7°W, to be applied to all bearings before they can be laid off on the chart.

It is usually sufficiently accurate to estimate the deviation from the card by eye, but for those who like to be very exact here is the method:

Find the compass course to steer to make a course of 210°T if the variation is 6°W.

$$\begin{array}{ll}\text{Course} & 210°\text{T} \\ \text{Variation} & 6°\text{W} \\ \hline \text{Course} & 216°\text{M} \end{array}$$

206°M gives a deviation of 6°E.
229°M gives a deviation of 9°E.
∴ in 23° change of course the deviation changes 3°

∴ in 1° change of course the deviation changes $\dfrac{3}{23}$°

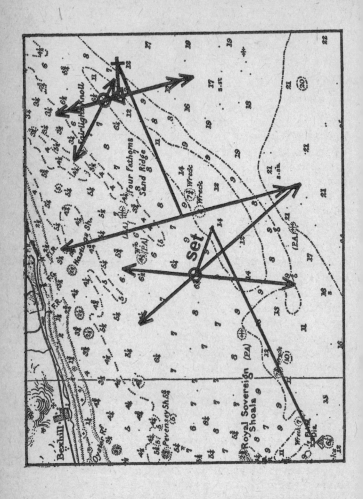

∴ for 216° — 206° = 10° change of course the deviation

changes $\dfrac{3 \times 10}{23} = 1\frac{1}{3}°$

∴ the deviation for 216°M is $7\frac{1}{3}$°E.

$$
\begin{array}{ll}
\text{Course} & 216°\text{M} \\
\text{Deviation} & 7\frac{1}{3}°\text{E} \\
\hline
\text{Course} & 208\frac{2}{3}°\text{C}
\end{array}
$$

A few chapters ago, just as we were setting out for Treport, I said that we were ready to go except for one thing, but we went anyway. The one thing I meant was a card of deviations so now we have one and we can go anywhere.

I hope I didn't keep you in suspense with this secretive approach. Let us now set off again. It will be necessary in the future to refer to the deviation card, so put a marker in the page.

Dover Strait Chart No. 5116
Variation 6°W

(1) Using the deviation card, find the compass courses to steer from the Royal Sovereign Lt. V. to a position 2 miles 180°T from Dungeness Lt. Ho., thence to a position 2 miles 180°T from Folkestone Gp. Fl. Lt. thence to the Varne Buoy, thence to a position one mile 270°T from C. Griz Nez Lt. Find also the distance on each course.

The degree of precision required by the Ministry of Transport is $\frac{1}{2}$°, which means that the deviation must be worked out to the nearest $\frac{1}{2}$°.

(2) Leaving the Royal Sovereign Lt. V. the log was set at zero, and when it showed 7 Bexhill Church bore 334°C and Hastings Church 018°C. Find the vessel's position and the set and drift of the current experienced.

Method:

From our previous calculation in Qu. I the error of the compass on the 1st course is 14°W.

Bexhill Ch.	334°C		Hastings Ch.	018°C
Comp. Error	14°W		Comp. Error	14°W
	320°T			004°T

Method:

Royal Sovereign to Dungeness	Dungeness to Folkestone	Folkestone to the Varne	The Varne to C. Gris Nez
063 T	040 T	106 T	140 T
Var. 6 W	6 W	6 W	6 W
069 M	046 M	112 M	146 M
Dev. 8 W	5 W	7 W	2 W
077 C	051 C	119 C	148 C
Dist. 22.2 Miles	13 Miles	7.2 Miles	11 Miles

When we lay these bearings off on the chart they cross in the position Lat. 50°46′.3 N, Long. 0°34′.8E.

Now measure 7 miles along the course line from the Lt. V. This gives the D.R. position and the direction from this position to the fix is the set of the current, the distance from D.R. to fix the drift.

Set. 290°T. Drift 1.4 miles

(3) With the vessel's head on a course of 080°C Hastings Church bore 359°C, log 8, and one hour later when the log read 13, the same Church bore 312°C. Find the position of the vessel on the 2nd bearing allowing for a current setting 270°T at 1 knot.

Method:

Consulting the deviation card we find that a compass course of 080° gives a deviation of 8°W. This, in combination with the variation of 6°W makes the compass error 14°W.

Course	080°C	Bearings	359°C	312°C
C. Error	14°W	Bearings	14°W	14°W
	066°T		345°T	298°T

Lay off the first bearing 345°T through Hastings Church. From anywhere on this first bearing lay off the course 066°T and measure 5 miles along it. This gives the D.R. position. From the D.R. position lay off the current 270°T for 1 mile. This gives the estimated position. Through the estimated position lay off a line parallel to the first bearing. This is the transferred position line. Through Hastings Church lay off the second bearing 298°T, and the point where this bearing cuts the transferred position line is the vessel's position on the second bearing.

Lat. 50°49′.2N, Long. 0°43′E.

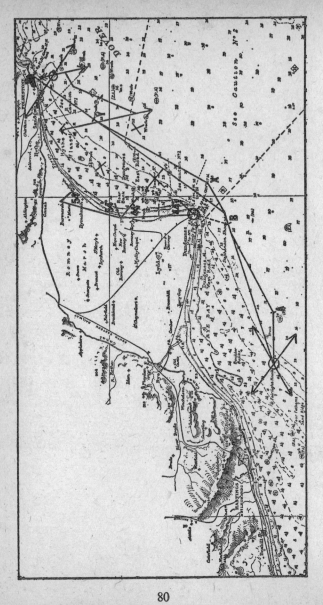

This large motor yacht is equipped
with radar, an instrument of great
help to the navigator if properly used.

Two echo sounders suitable for yachtsmen;
below by Pye and opposite by BEME.
These instruments give accurate depth readings.

Two types of small ships' compasses.

Two instruments of help to
the small vessel under sail –
a wind direction indicator and a
wind speed indicator. Both
operate through mast head fittings.

Aground in Gurnard Bay during a race.
Good navigation is as important when
racing as at any other time.

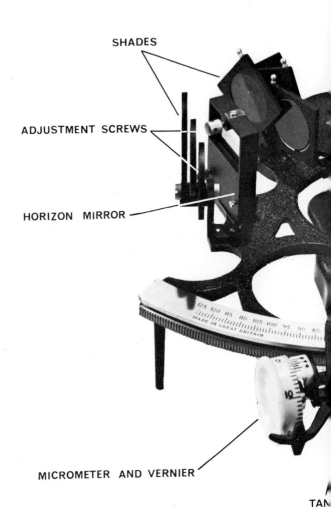

SHADES

ADJUSTMENT SCREWS

HORIZON MIRROR

MICROMETER AND VERNIER

TAN

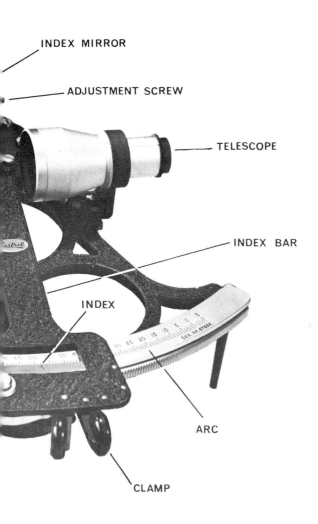

INDEX MIRROR

ADJUSTMENT SCREW

TELESCOPE

INDEX BAR

INDEX

ARC

CLAMP

SCREW

Coastal navigation demands a clear view, and it is essential to keep the windscreens of enclosed cockpits free of spray and rain. Below is a car-type wiper made by Dudley Marine, and opposite the circular revolving screen made by George Kent.

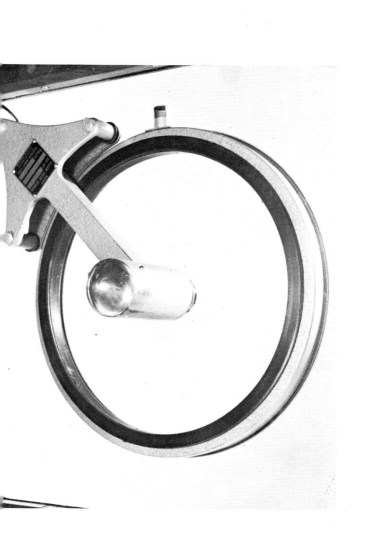

Top: A radio telephone set by Coastal radio,
covering standard broadcast bands and navigational
bands for Consul and direction finding.
Below: an American range finder
sold in the U.K. by Mansell & Fisher.

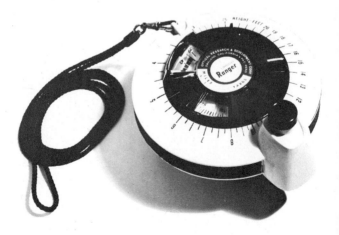

Using a radio direction finder in
the cabin of a yacht fully
equipped with Brookes & Gatehouse
electronic navigation devices.

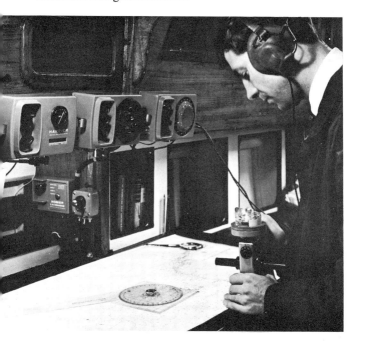

Instrument layout in cockpit of a
motor cruiser. The compass sited
near metal, will have to be adjusted
and a table of deviations made out.

Cockpit of a BOB 8-metre cruising catamaran.
The compass is well placed above the wheel,
and Shoreway echo sounder and Sumlog log
are easily read by the helmsman.

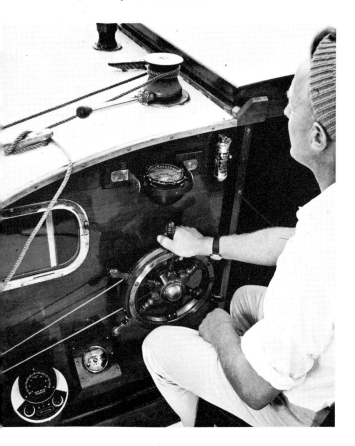

The small sloop 'Penny Ballerina' in
which Geoffrey Godwin navigated his
way across the Atlantic single handed.
Note the log top left, and 'Bosun' compass.

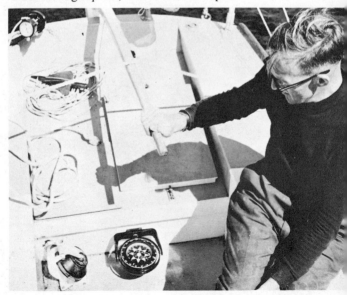

CHAPTER SIXTEEN

FURTHER PROBLEMS

Dover Strait Chart No. 5116
Variation 6°W

(1) Approaching Dungeness Lt. off Rye Bay with the vessel's head 080°C, Fairlight Church bore 323°C and Dungeness Lt. bore 075°C. Using the deviation card in the previous chapter, find the ship's position.

Find the compass course to steer from this position to a position with Dungeness Lt. Ho. bearing 000°T at a distance of 2 miles to counteract the effect of a current setting 090°T at 2 knots, vessel's speed 4 knots. Give also the true bearing and distance of Dungeness Lt. Ho. after 1½ hours on this course, and the distance made good towards the destination.

Method :—The deviation for the ship's head 080°C is 8°W. This makes the compass error 14°W when taken in conjunction with the variation of 6°W.

	Fairlight Ch.	Dungeness
	323°C	075°C
C. Error	14°W	14°W
	309°T	061°T

Lay off these two bearings on the chart and the position will be found to be in Lat. 50°49.8′N, Long. 0°44′E.

From this position draw a line on the chart to the destination 2 miles due South of Dungeness Lt. This is the course to be made good. From the fix lay off the current 090°T and measure 3 miles along it for the distance the ship will drift in 1½ hours, to A. Next take 6 miles on the dividers for the distance steamed on 1½ hours, and with centre A cut the course to be made good at B.

AB is the course to steer to counteract the current, and the ship will be at B after 1½ hours.

Course to steer	061°T
Variation	6°W

	067°M
Deviation	8°W

Course to steer	075°C

After 1½ hours Dungeness bore 018°T distant 2.4 miles. Distance made good towards the destination is 8.8 miles.

---

(2) From a position 2 miles due South True of Dungeness Lt. No. find the compass course to steer to Folkestone Gp. F. Lt. to counteract the effect of a current setting 060°T at 1 knot, ship's speed 4 knots, and state what would be the effective speed.

Method:—Draw a line from the position off Dungeness to Folkestone Lt. This is the course to be made good and from the position off Dungeness lay off the current 060°T for a distance of 2 miles (2 hours).

From this Eastern end of the current measure 8 miles with the dividers back on to the course to be made good, to Y. XY is the required course and the distance from the position off Dungeness to Y is the distance made good in 2 hours. This distance divided by 2 will give the effective speed, i.e. the distance made good in 1 hour. Speed made good 4.9 knots.

True course to steer	030°T
Variation	6°W

	036°M
Deviation	4°W

	040°C

---

(3) Some time later the horizontal angle between Dungeness Lt. Ho. and the tower marked on the coast East of New Romney was observed to be 46°, and that between the same tower and Burmarsh Church 36°. Find the ship's position, and if Dungeness Lt. bore 246°C, find the deviation for the direction of the ship's head.

Method: In the absence of a station pointer join Dungeness Lt. Ho. to the tower by a line, and at each end of this line construct an angle of 44° (the complement of 46° i.e. 90° – 46°) on the seaward side. With centre where these two lines cross and radius to the tower, describe the arc of a circle to seaward. This is part of one position circle.

Next join the tower to church and at each end construct an angle of 54° (90° – 36°) to seaward. With centre where these two lines cross and radius to the tower describe an arc to seaward to cut the first arc. This second arc is part of another position circle. If the vessel is somewhere on both arcs she must be at the point where they cross. I make it Lat. 50°48′.1N, Long. 1°6′5E. The true bearing of Dungeness Lt. from this position was 237° measured on the chart, which with a variation of 6°W gives a deviation of 3°W when compared to the observed compass bearing.

---

(4) A conspicuous clump behind Hythe bore 357°C with the vessel heading 033°C. One hour later the same clump bore 315°C. Find the distance of the vessel from Folkestone Lt. Ho. at this time allowing for the spring tide given in Table C at 2 hours after H.W. at Dover, the vessel's speed being 4 knots. Deviation as given on the deviation card.

Method:

Ship's head	033°C
Deviation	3°W
	030°
Variation	6°W
Course	024°T

83

1st bearing	357°C	2nd bearing	315°C
Course Error	9°W	Course Error	9°W
	348°T		306°T

Inspecting Tide Table C, it is found that at the given time the tide is setting 056°T at 1 knot at Spring tides.

Lay off the two bearings through the conspicuous clump. From any point on the 1st bearing, lay off the course of 024°T for 4 miles and from the end of these 4 miles lay off the tide for 1 mile.

Through the end of the current draw a line parallel to the first bearing. Where this line cuts the second bearing will be the vessel's required position. This should be found to be 1.3 miles from Folkestone Lt. Ho.

Bad Visibility fixes

If the visibility becomes bad it is possible to get some idea of one's position by taking soundings at intervals and plotting these on the chart. Let us take an example to show what I mean.

A vessel in D.R. position Lat. 50°37′N, Long. 1°00′E took a sounding at 0200 in 13 fathoms. Steering a course of 090°T at a speed of 4 knots she obtained the following soundings:

0215	8	fathoms
0245	5½	fathoms
0345	18	fathoms f.s.
0400	20	fathoms
0430	10	fathoms
0445	4	fathoms s. sh

The exercise is to find the ship's position when the last sounding was taken at 0445.

Method: First plot the D.R. position on the chart. Now look around this position for a sounding of 13 fathoms. There is one to the south and one to the east and one to the south west, but since the soundings get rapidly less at first it seems more likely to be the one to the east. Let us start from there then and draw in the course of 090°T.

It is now necessary to work out the distances run to each sounding and this should be done in each case from the 0200 position, i.e.:

0215	1	mile
0245	3	miles
0345	7	miles
0400	8	miles
0430	10	miles
0445	11	miles

Measure these distances along the course from the 0200 position, and see if the soundings taken correspond to those on the chart. It will be found that from the position we have chosen they do, and so we can assume that at 0445 we are on the "4" mark near the N. end of the Vergoyer Bank.

Notice that, by arming the lead and getting a sample of the bottom when a sounding is taken, the position is further verified. This is the great advantage of sounding by leadline.

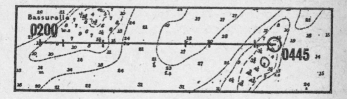

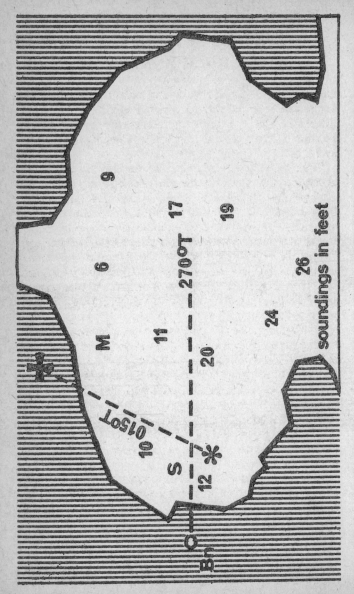

soundings in feet

CHAPTER SEVENTEEN

ANCHORING

One great advantage of a fix by horizontal angles, is that the angles can be found very simply by the difference between the bearings taken on any compass, and the accuracy of the position obtained is not affected by the compass error, whatever it is.

When the angles are taken by a sextant the fix is even more accurate as the value of each angle is made more precise.

I have explained how to lay off this kind of fix on the chart by practical geometry. When you can do this, it is an accurate and simple method. A rather more expensive method is by means of a station pointer. This is a three armed instrument, two of the arms being movable. The latter are set to the observed angles one on each side of the centre fixed arm, and when the bevelled edge of each arm is on its respective point on the chart, the centre from which the arms radiate will give the position.

A third, and much simpler way, is to draw the angles on tracing paper, place this over the chart and manipulate it so that the lines cross the points observed. The point from which the lines begin will then be the ship's position.

This is an excellent method of finding the position of the vessel at anchor, too, and having fixed the position of the ship by this means at any time, a compass error can be obtained by comparing the compass bearing of one of the points with the true bearing of the same point from the position on the chart.

It might be a good idea at this juncture to say something about anchoring. This is often necessary in a strange place, and there are various things to look out for when selecting an anchorage.

The selection, with one or two alternatives, should be made before you reach the vicinity in which it is intended to anchor, and such things should be taken into account as the depth of water, the kind of bottom, the direction and strength of tidal streams, the length of ship, the prevailing wind and its probable strength, and the draught of the ship.

The prevailing wind in Great Britain is westerly, and stronger winds may be expected in winter than in summer. It is, therefore, better to find a bay which is protected from the westwards, and it is better to anchor on the west side of such a bay. In the usual passage of a depression, when storms occur, the wind increases in a south-west direction, gradually veering to west and north-west, and dying out in that direction.

This is not always so, but is very often so.

Having decided, then, to anchor to windward, look at the kind of bottom described on the chart. The best types of holding ground are clay, mud and sand, while rock, shingle and shell are poor types of holding ground. So look for a place with a nice sandy bottom, for, while clay and mud hold a little better, you can catch fish on sand. Just a thought.

Make sure that there is plenty of water for you to remain afloat. If you are drawing, say, 5 feet of water, then I would say you want at least 2 fathoms or 12 feet of water marked on the chart. This will mean that you will always have at least 6 feet of water below the keel and generally more, depending on the rise and fall of the tide.

Make sure that there are no rocks or other obstructions near, and remember to allow for the length of the chain when calculating the radius of swing. The amount of chain to be paid out is usually about eight times the depth of water, which is 100 feet for a depth of 12 feet of water, so that if the vessel is 30 feet long she is really 130 feet from the anchor and this is her radius of swing.

There must be clear water inside this circle, and a bit outside it too. It should be remembered that in a strong wind she may drag her anchor, so allow yourself plenty of distance to windward of obstructions.

Do not anchor inside a prohibited area. This will be clearly marked on the chart. If by some mischance you ever pick up a cable or power line on your anchor, pass an ordinary manila rope round the cable and make fast, then lower the anchor down a bit until it comes clear. Heave it right up and then let one end of the rope go in which the cable is hanging. This will return the cable to the bottom of the sea. Note your position at the time of this occurrence and notify the authorities, for the cable may be damaged.

If the anchor is twisted into the cable so that it is difficult to free it, the thing to do is to put a buoy on the anchor, slip it, and report to the authorities, who will recover your anchor for you when they sight their cable.

You mustn't cut the cable, for it may be a power line and you will be electrocuted.

I feel that there may be a certain amount of expense in all this, and some of it will probably devolve on you, though not perhaps in a case of pure accident or stress of weather. But play it safe and don't foul a cable if at all possible.

It may be that while you are at anchor you will want to go ashore, so anchor near a landing place.

Bearing all these things in mind, then, the anchorages should be selected and a conspicuous object chosen as a leading mark to the desired position in each case. The bearing from the mark through the anchorage should be such that it makes a clear run in when approaching. When you get close enough, pick out something in transit with the principal mark, not necessarily marked on the chart, and keep them in line by running in on the transit.

A second bearing should be obtained as nearly at right angles to the transit as possible. Here again a suitable mark or transit should be chosen; and its bearing watched as you come in on the transit ahead. When the beam bearing is getting close to that desired, slow right down, and let go the anchor when both bearings agree with those worked out from the chosen position on the chart.

If it happens that there is another vessel anchored there already, then you will have to go to one of your other selected positions.

When actually letting go the anchor, you should have slight sternway over the ground, which is often different from slight sternway through the water.

Your relationship to the ground can be ascertained by

watching transit bearings on either side, and if there is any tide you should always come to an anchor heading into it or "stemming" it. The water has a much greater effect on a vessel than the wind, and the wind must be very strong to overcome the effect of the tide.

In a strong wind a vessel riding to a single anchor will yaw from side to side. At the end of each sheer, the chain comes tight and pulls her head round on the other sheer. It is at this point that the anchor could break out of the ground and start to drag. If this is likely to happen, it is better to let go a second anchor and slack away on both chains rather than to slack away on the single chain.

To let go the second anchor, wait until she is at the end of her sheer away from the anchor that is out and then let go the other one and slack away on both. If the anchors are well spread this will also help to stop her from sheering about so much.

The port anchor is called the working anchor on the northern hemisphere, and is the one that should be used at single anchor. This is so that if you have to let go the second anchor you will find that as the wind shifts to the right, or veers, the anchor chains will not cross each other, nor will you get a turn in them.

And it is very important to heave in the second anchor again when the wind drops, or you will get a turn in the cables.

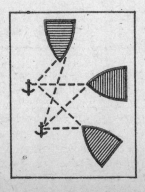

CHAPTER EIGHTEEN

FINDING DISTANCE

Pukka navigators find their distance off a point of land of known height by observing the angle of elevation of the point by means of a sextant.

I will not go into the mechanics of a sextant, but by means of this instrument the top of the point may be superimposed on the water's edge, and the vertical angle so measured may be read off on the scale in degrees and minutes of arc. The said navigators then fly to a table called "Distance off by vertical sextant angle" from which, with the vertical angle and the height of the observed point as arguments, they extract their distance from the point in nautical miles and cables.

This table solves a right-angled plane triangle. Those of my readers with a knowledge of right-angled plane trigonometry will see immediately how this solution can be arrived at by calculation, and those without such a knowledge will take my word for it, because they believe, and rightly, that in spite of a somewhat flippant manner on occasion, I would not mislead them.

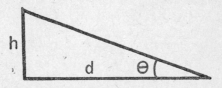

If h = the height of the point in feet, $\theta°$ (Theta) = the vertical angle and d = the distance off the point, then
$$d = h \text{ cotangent } \theta°$$
The answer, being in feet, should be divided by 6000 to convert it to miles.

For the ordinary amateur navigator this is a very difficult procedure, for he generally does not possess a sextant, or, possessing one, he is very unsure of its manipulation and so, as far as he is concerned, the compilation of such a table as "Distance off by vertical sextant angle" is so much wasted effort.

This is a pity, for the use of a sextant ensures maximum accuracy, but I am full of sympathy for the sextantless sailor and I will now outline a method of finding the distance off a point of known height by the use of very simple materials indeed.

If you take an ordinary ruler graduated in tenths or eighths of an inch, and hold it out at arm's length in front of you, as you see an artist doing sometimes with his brush to check the proportions of his model, you will find that the ruler is 25 inches from your eye. Try it.

With the ruler held thus, measure the height of the point of land in tenths of an inch and the distance you are from the point can then by found by solving similar triangles, as I will show you. If you are unable to follow the working out of the solution it does not matter, but do remember the solution itself.

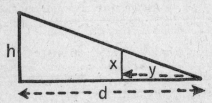

in the figure h = the height of the point of land
  d = the distance off the point of land
  y = 25 inches
  x = the measurement of "h" in tenths of an inch.

Here we have two similar triangles in which

$$\frac{d}{h} = \frac{y}{x}$$

$$\therefore d = \frac{hy}{x}$$

Now we must bring all the constituents on the right hand

side of the equation to the same units, "h" being in feet we multiply it by 12 to bring it to inches, and "x" being in tenths of an inch, to bring it to inches we must divide it by 10.

$$\therefore \ d = \frac{12hy}{X/10} = \frac{120hy}{X} = \frac{120x25xh}{X}$$

$$\text{inches} = \frac{120x25xh}{12x6000xX} \text{ Miles.}$$

When we work this out it is found that:

$$\text{Distance off the point} = \frac{h}{24X}, \text{ or}$$

$$\frac{\text{The height of the point in feet.}}{24 \text{ x the measure of the point in } 1/10''}$$

In plain language, to find your distance off a point of land of known height, divide the height of the point in feet by 24 and again by the number of tenths of an inch it measures on a ruler held at a distance of 25 inches from the eye. Here is an example:

A lighthouse whose height is given on the chart as 120 feet measures 2/10″ on a ruler held at a distance of 25 inches from the eye. Find the distance off the lighthouse in miles.

$$d = \frac{h}{24X} = \frac{120}{24x2} = 2.5 \text{ miles}$$

Of course, if you have a good steady hand and measure the height of the lighthouse in sixteenths of an inch, then the equation becomes

$$d = \frac{h}{15x}$$

"x" this time being the number of sixteenths of an inch in the height measurement.

When the distance off a point of land is known, it means that the position line, that is the line passing through the ship's position, is the circle drawn with the point as centre and the distance off as radius. If the distances off two points are known and the two positions' circles drawn, then the ship is at one of the intersections of the two circles, Drawing A. You must select the correct intersection of course but it will generally be obvious which one that is.

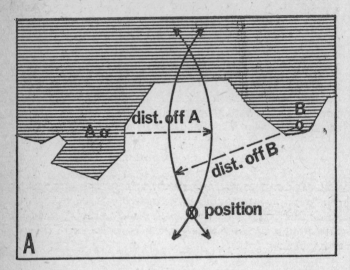

A position can also be obtained by a bearing and distance from a point. Any kind of point may be used, a lighthouse, a beacon, a church, a flagstaff or even a mountain, so long as the height of the point is known. Unless the point is very close and great accuracy is necessary, no allowance need be made for the state of the tide.

The height of an object is always given above Mean High Water Springs so that usually it is higher above the water than the height given. This means that when the height is measured to the water's edge by ruler or sextant, the distance off by calculation will be less than it is in reality. This is an advantage, as it will make you pull out sooner if you are too close.

This kind of information is, to use a well known phrase, worth a guinea a box, if I may say so in all modesty, but it can be taken a step further, for, by means of a simple transposition, it is possible to find the measurement on the ruler necessary to pass a given distance off a point of known height.

This is made use of when there is an unmarked danger off a point which is to be avoided, and the equation then becomes $X = \dfrac{h}{15d}$ when X is in sixteenths of an inch.

Let us say that 1 mile off a lighthouse 120 feet high there is a dangerous wreck and it is desired to pass this danger at a distance of one mile, in which case the lighthouse must be passed at a distance of two miles. Drawing B. The measurements of the light in sixteenths of an inch at this distance

$$= \frac{120}{15\times2} = 4 \text{ sixteenths.}$$

If, as you are coming up to the light it measures four sixteenths of an inch before it comes abeam, bring the light abeam and keep it abeam until you are back on your original course again, by which time you will be passing the danger at the required distance.

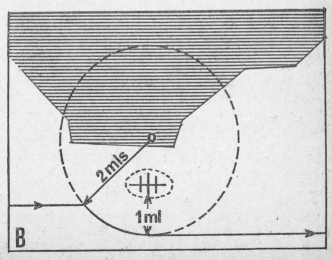

CHAPTER NINETEEN

RADIO AIDS

In the silence of the open sea, silent except for the sighing of the wind and the swish of the water, we are surrounded by a cacophony of sound. To prove this, all you have to do is to switch on a radio and the whole world will come in.

We take this very much for granted nowadays, even those of us who remember when it all began, and we think that there is nothing unusual in hearing someone speak from the other side of the world, nor do we marvel very much when we are told of radio aids to navigation which will give our position within yards.

Most yachtsmen feel that this kind of navigation is outside their financial scope, however, and it is to these that this article is directed. For among all this welter of signals there is a system of position fixing which bleeps away twenty-four hours a day from three different stations, a system which will give a position within miles, not yards, but which is very valuable, nevertheless. It is called Consol.

Once upon a time it was said of Banks that they would lend you money if you could prove you didn't need it. The same could be said of Consol, that it will give you a position when you don't need it. It is no use if you happen to want it to enter a harbour in fog, but if you are out of sight of land it will give a position sufficiently accurate to shape a course for some recognizable land mark.

Using this system in the east end of London I have had a fix as far away as Greenford, and using it in Romford have been located in Dartford. This seems funny to Londoners, but to those outside London it is all London and the error negligible. And so it is, for in the one case the error in position was 12 miles, and in the other case 7 miles, which is not a great error if you are in the middle of the North Sea.

Consol is a long range navigational aid with a range of 700 miles in daylight over land and 1,000 miles over water, 1,200 miles at night. It was instituted by the Germans during the last war, and improved on, by us since.

There are five transmitting stations – Stavanger in Norway, Bushmills in Northern Ireland, Ploneis in France just behind Ushant, Lugo in Spain just behind Finisterre, and Seville just west of Gibraltar. The first three named work continuously.

THE APPARATUS

All the apparatus needed is a medium frequency radio receiver. It is not really as simple as that because the wave bands for Consol are between the medium and long wave broadcast bands and it is not always possible to hear them on an ordinary radio, but try the top end of the medium wave band for Stavanger which has a frequency of 319 K/cs. (940 metres). Its call sign is LEC in Morse, dot dash dot dot, dot, dash dot dash dot, in English, and this is followed by a long dash and then a series of dots (or dashes) merging into a continuous tone and emerging again as a series of dashes (or dots).

Count the number of dashes and the number of dots in a complete cycle, add them together, and their sum should be 60. If it is not, add half the difference from 60 to each one, i.e., 22 dots-34 dashes, the sum is 56. Difference from 60 is 4. Add the half of four to each so that the correct count is 24 dots-36 dashes. Do this several times until you get the same count repeating itself.

LINES OF BEARING

It is necessary when fixing the position to get counts from two different stations. The lines of bearing from the transmitting stations are printed over charts published by the Hydrographic Office. These lines are distinguished by the number of the first characteristic in the count, that is, in the case of the example I gave, 24 dots.

The same characteristic count is repeated in different bearings on the chart, but it is usually fairly easy to pick out the appropriate line of bearing for your position, which is

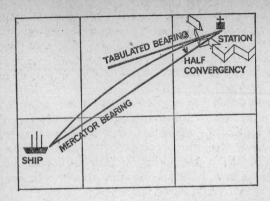

where the bearings from the two stations cross. It is also possible to fix the position on a chart which is not over-printed. This is done by the aid of tables of bearings given in the Admiralty List of Radio Signals. Vol. 5, or more conveniently in a booklet C.A.P. 59, "Consol," published by H.M.S.O. at 3s.* The use of the tables is fully explained, and in fact there is a full explanation of Consol and its use.

Because of the inherent limitations of the system there are no large scale Consol charts.

Chart No. L2339 covers the whole of the North Sea and No. L2 the British Isles. A full list is given in the Admiralty Chart Catalogue, which should be consulted so that you get the chart most suitable for your district. These Consol charts cost 10s. each and are much easier to use than the tables of bearings for ordinary charts. If you are going to do any cruising, it is well worth getting the relevant chart so that you can use this method of position fixing.

Here is a list of the frequencies:

Stavanger	LEC	319	K/cs	940	metres
Bushmills	MWN	266	K/cs	1128	metres
Ploneis	TRQ	257	K/cs	1167	metres
Lugo		303	K/cs	990	metres
Seville		311	K/cs	965	metres

*Subject to Amendment No. 1, 4d. extra.

Consol is as accurate as Radio Direction Finding, for they experience the same advantages and disadvantages, with the balance heavily on the side of Consol. For the Consol bearings are independent of the ship's compass, and the apparatus sending the signals out is continually monitored by skilled personnel.

When a radio signal passes between two points on the earth's surface it takes the shortest route, which is along what is called a great circle. When drawn on a chart the great circle appears as a curve. If you are using the tables in the booklet to get your bearing from the Consol station a correction must be applied to change the curve into a straight line so that it can be laid off on the chart.

This correction is called the "half convergency" and it is tabulated for each Consol station, the arguments being your latitude and the difference of longitude between you and the station.

When the bearing is between 000 deg. and 180 deg. the correction is added. When the bearing is between 180 deg. and 360 deg. it is subtracted.

COASTAL NAVIGATION

Examples for Exercise
Using Deviation Card in the text and
Variation 6°W

(1) Find the compass courses to steer and the distance on each course from a position with Beachy Head Lt. bearing 000°T, distant 1 mile, to a position with the Royal Sovereign Lt. V. bearing 000°T, distant 1 mile, thence to the entrance to Treport.

(2) With the ship's head 140°C. Beachy Head bore 010°C at 0800 and at 0900 the Royal Sovereign Lt. V. bore 068°C. Ship's speed 5 K. and current setting 040°T at 1K. Find the ship's position at 0900.

(3) At 0830, log 12, with Beachy Head Lt. bearing 000°T at a distance of 1 mile a ship set a course of 080°C, and at 1000, log 20, Hastings Church bore 043°C and Bexhill Church 359°C. Find the ship's position and the set and drift of the current experienced.

(4) Find the compass course to steer from a position with the Royal Sovereign Lt. V. bearing 180°T, distant 3 miles, to a position with Dungeness Lt. bearing 000°T, distant 3 miles, to counteract a current setting 090°T at 1½ K, ship's speed 6 K, allowing 8° leeway for a Northerly wind. Give also the true bearing and distance of Dungeness Lt. after 2 hours.

(5) The following bearings were taken by a compass of unknown deviation:

Rye Harbour Entrance Fl. R. Lt.	347°
Gt. Cheyne Court	011°
Dungeness Lt.	058°

Find the ship's position and the deviation of the compass for the direction of the ship's head.

(6) Find the compass courses to steer and the distance on each course from a position with Dungeness Lt. bearing 270°T distant 1 mile to the Gp. Fl. Lt. at Folkestone, thence to South Sand Head Lt. Vessel.

(7) With the ship's head 260°C the South Sand Head Lt. V. bore 319°C and 45 minutes later it bore 045°C. During

this time the tide was setting 030°T at 1 K, ship's speed 4 K. Find the bearing and distance of the South Foreland Lt. at the time of taking the second bearing.

(8) Find the compass course to steer from the South Sand Head Lt. V. to the Varne Buoy to counteract a current setting 040°T at 2 K, ship's speed 6 K. Allow 7° leeway for a strong S.E. wind and state the time of arrival at the buoy, having left the Lt. V. at 0900 hours.

(9) A vessel left the Varne Buoy at 1200 hours, steering 146°C at a speed of 6 K. at 1330 hours. C. Gris Nez Lt. bore 183°C and Wissant Church 138°C. State the ship's position and the set and drift of the current experienced.

(10) Going from Dover to Calais the following horizontal angles were observed.
Calais Gp. Fl. Lt. 58° Air Gp. Fl. Lt. 54° C. Gris Nez Lt. Find the ship's Latitude and Longitude and if the Air Lt. bore 154° by the compass find the deviation of the compass for the direction of the ship's head.

(11) Find the compass courses to steer and the distance on each course from the Varne Buoy to a position 0.5 miles due East of the B.W. Bell Buoy at the North end of the Bassure de Baas, thence to the R.W. Buoy at the mouth of the R. Canche.

(12) With the ship's head 176°C, C. Gris Nez Lt. bore 132°C and a sounding gave 20 fathoms. After running for 6 miles by the log from this position the Occ. R. Lt. on Boulogne B'kwater bore 192°C and a B.W. Bell Buoy bore 312°C. Find the ship's position and the set and drift of the current experienced.

(13) At 0900 hrs. with the ship's head on 223°C Folkestone Qu. Fl. Lt. bore 267°C, log 67, and thirty minutes later it bore 337°C. log 70. The tide was estimated to be setting 056°T, at 1 K. Find the ship's position at 0930.

(14) Find the compass course to steer from the Varne Buoy to pass 1 mile off Dungeness Lt. to counteract a tide setting 031°T at 2 K, ship's speed 6 K and allow 5° leeway for a fresh N wind. Give also the bearing and distance of the lighthouse after 2 hours.

101

(15) In Dungeness East Roads the following horizontal angles were observed:

Dungeness Lt. 71° Burmarsh Church 46° Conspicuous Clump.
Find the ship's position.

(16) Find the compass courses to steer and the distance to steam on each course from a position with Dungeness Lt. Ho. bearing 000°T distant 1 miles to Hastings Flashing Red Lt., thence to the Royal Sovereign Lt. V.

(17) Find the compass course to steer from the Royal Sovereign Lt. V. to Hastings F. R. Lt. to counteract the effect of a current setting 248°T at 2 K, ship's speed 5 K, and allow 5° leeway for a NW wind. State also the distance made good towards the destination in 2 hours.

(18) From the Royal Sovereign Lt. V. a ship steered 283°C at 6 K and after one hour Beachy Head bore 267°C and Eastbourne F.G. Lt. bore 343°C. Find the set and rate of the current.

(19) With the ship's head 004°C at 1230 hours Dungeness Lt. Ho. bore 348°C, log 62, and at 1300, log 65 the same Lt. Ho. bore 316°C. The tide was estimated to be setting 211°T at 1 K. Find the position at 1300 hours.

(20) In the Dover Channel the following horizontal angles were obtained, Folkestone Gp. Fl. Lt. 70° Fl. Lt. on Dover B'kwater 21° S. Foreland Lt. Find the ship's position.

PART II ASTRO NAVIGATION

INTRODUCTION

It is one thing to be able to navigate in coastal waters where, as we have seen in the first part of this book, it is usually possible to check the accuracy of one's position by fixes taken from landmarks. Or, if all else fails, by arming the lead and cross-referring from depth and type of bottom with the chart.

Out of sight of land, however, with the deeps of ocean beneath the keel and no static objects from which to take bearings, it is essential to have other means of finding one's position. Luckily, the sun and other heavenly bodies follow closely calculated courses, and the art of astro-navigation enables the mariner to pin point his position with reasonable accuracy anywhere in the world.

CHAPTER TWENTY

ASTRONOMY AND ALL THAT

Astro-navigation is the art of navigating by means of the heavenly bodies, the Sun, the Moon, the Planets, and the stars.

Men have always used these bodies for navigation, but for a long time this kind of plotting was very approximate and it was not until Harrison made his chronometer and enabled the mariner to keep exact time to the nearest second at sea that astro-navigation really became reliable as we know it today.

Even today, however, it is not an exact science, because it makes use of one factor at least, and comes under the influence of several others, which cannot be computed exactly.

To the ordinary man in the street, and even to the extraordinary man in a small boat, I suppose that the very sound of astro-navigation is as mysterious as astrology, even if its results are more dependable. He probably thinks that it is impossible for him to understand it without a great deal of study.

This is true beyond a certain point, but up to that point understanding astro-navigation is just common sense. To learn it, all that is needed is the ability to read. To do it, the ability to add and subtract.

I hope to make it so easy for you to get a position that in a small boat jumping up and down in the middle of the Atlantic you will be able to take the altitudes of two stars and work out a position to within 10 miles of where you actually are, in half an hour.

When you consider that the Atlantic is 3,000 miles across and you are doing perhaps six knots it seems to me that this is sufficiently accurate.

From this extreme case to the other in which you are standing on a steady platform taking the altitudes of the Sun and Moon at the same time, I can offer you the possibility of a position in five minutes to within a mile.

With a little application you can become a much better navigator than, for instance, Columbus, Drake or Raleigh, thanks to Harrison, Lord Kelvin, Marconi, and Her Majesty's Stationery Office.

The Board of Trade requirements for a certificate of competency as Yachtmaster Coastal are, in this respect, that you should be able to find the time of sunset and sunrise, moonset and moonrise on any day and in any place, and to find the true bearing of the Sun at any time when it is on or above the horizon.

This is for sailing only within coastal limits. The Official Home Trade limits are the coasts of the British Isles and that of the Continent between Elbe and Brest, but for Home Trade Certificates professional seamen are obliged to be able to find Latitude and Longitude by observations of celestial bodies.

It is therefore not too much to say that even when navigating quite close to our shores the ability to find a reasonable position by "taking sights" could be very useful.

And anyway, astro-navigation is interesting in itself – to be able to fix your position anywhere in the world with nothing in sight but the sky. I took sights night and morning for years and the interest in seeing the result never waned.

It is quite possible that many of my readers have the knowledge necessary for working out the Longitude and all they need is to be shown how this knowledge is applied to the problem. For it may be said that astro-navigation consists in the solution of a spherical triangle, given its three sides, to find an angle, or given two sides and the contained angle, to find the third side.

If this kind of talk frightens you I hasten to add that there are pre-computed tables which do the calculations for you and all you have to do is to look them up. It will be one of my aims to try to get you to understand what you are doing, but this is not imperative.

It is interesting, however, to know something about astronomy and the principles of astro-navigation.

Let us begin with the universe. The latest reports say that this is a vast space having in it at widely spaced intervals what are known as galaxies.

Each galaxy is a collection of stars grouped in such shapes as spirals, dinner plates, soup plates and saucers.

The size of the universe is infinite. The distance between each galaxy is unthinkable, the size of each galaxy is incredible, the distance between the stars in a galaxy is unimaginable and the stars themselves colossal, some being more colossal than others, some less. I feel that this is the only safe way to talk about these things. It is all rather frightening but there is nothing we can do about it and it has been going on for ages.

Our own Sun is a star in one of these galaxies. This galaxy is saucer-shaped and the Sun is one of the smaller stars in it and placed towards the outer edge of the saucer, ordinarily and inconspicuously.

The rest of the stars in our galaxy are those we see in the sky at night. When we look in a certain direction we see a band of stars which we call the "Milky Way."

This effect is due to the fact that when looking in this direction we are looking across the saucer-shape where the stars are most numerous.

If we look in a direction at right angles to the Milky Way we are looking out of the saucer and the stars are more widely spaced.

Having narrowed our field of enquiry from infinity down to a mere galaxy, we will continue the process and get down to these bodies in the heavens which can be useful to us. Not many, I may say.

CHAPTER TWENTY-ONE

THE HEAVENLY BODIES

The Sun is the centre of the Solar system, which consists of that body and a number of planets circling round it at various distances from it. They are Mercury, Venus, Earth, Mars, Jupiter, Saturn, Uranus, Neptune and Pluto in that order working outwards from the Sun.

Between Mars and Jupiter there are a number of very small planets called Asteroids. Only four of the major planets are visible to the naked eye from the earth, namely Venus, Jupiter, Mars and Saturn, and these are the only ones used for navigation.

The Solar system is one way only. All the planets go round the Sun in the same direction and on roughly the same plane, and several of them have satellites of their own called moons, and these also go round their planets in the same direction as the planets go round the Sun. The Earth has one moon, Mars has two, Jupiter has eight and Saturn 10.

The Earth takes a year to go right round the Sun. Mars takes two of our years to go round the Sun and Jupiter takes 12 of our years.

This accounts for the changing positions of the planets against the stars, because our relative positions are changing all the time and to help us find them you look for a bright star where no bright star should be and that is a planet. Simple.

This is not the only way to locate planets, of course, but it is useful.

It is possible indeed to work out quite easily the bearing and altitude of any celestial body at any time, so that to find it, all you have to do is to look in that direction at that height, and there it will be. The only hazard to this kind of thing is cloud.

As the earth goes round the Sun it also turns on its axis

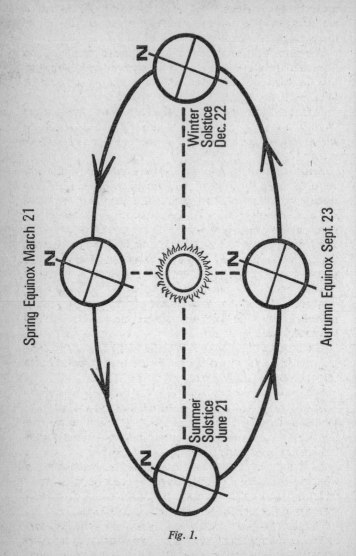

Fig. 1.

108

and each revolution takes 24 hours. It is this revolution which causes night and day, since for half the 24 hours we are facing the Sun and the other half we are on the side of the earth away from the Sun.

The path of the earth round the Sun is called its orbit and if we take the plane of this orbit to be horizontal, it appears that the axis about which the earth turns daily is not vertical, but tilted to an angle of $23\frac{1}{2}°$ to the vertical.

This is a fixed angle, and by a fortuitous circumstance there is a fairly prominent star directly above the North end of this axis permanently. This star is Polaris or the Pole star.

Before continuing with this simple exposition of the universe, to spike the guns of the purists and to reassure my readers in the face of harsh criticism, I have to confess that much of the information I have given you, and indeed will give you, is not strictly accurate.

For instance the Pole star is not directly above the pole, the earth actually takes $365\frac{1}{4}$ days to go round the Sun, the planets do not go round the Sun in circles, and so on.

These are all complications and will be overcome when they arise, if ever, but first I want you to get the general picture. I have your interests at heart and will not mislead you to any material extent.

The diagram (Fig. 1) gives a better idea of the earth orbiting the Sun and shows the tilt of the earth's axis. It also shows how the seasons are caused by the $23\frac{1}{2}°$ tilt.

Notice that at the equinoxes the Sun is directly above the equator and its declination is zero. At the Winter Solstice the Sun is directly over head in Lat. $23\frac{1}{2}°$ S and its declination is $23\frac{1}{2}°$S. At the summer solstice the Sun is directly overhead in Lat. $23\frac{1}{2}°$N and its declination is $23\frac{1}{2}°$N.

I will not give you the definition of declination, but this is what it means, that if you project the equator on to the sky – and this imaginary line is called the equinoctial – then declination is to the equinoctial as latitude is to the equator.

The sky of course is an imaginary roof over the universe, and it has been receding ever since it was first imagined, particularly in the last 50 years, until now its existence is doubted altogether, but on a clear day you can see it. It is called the celestial concave – the sky, to us.

Equinox means "equal night" and at the equinoxes the periods of daylight and darkness are equal all over the world.

Solstice means "sun sticks" and is the point at which the Sun stops and goes back again towards the equinoctial. At this time the periods of daylight and darkness vary considerably throughout the world, and in fact, some places have no light at all, and some no darkness, as you may see from (Fig. 2).

It can be seen that in our winter places above $66\frac{1}{2}°$N are in continuous darkness and above $66\frac{1}{2}°$S are in continuous daylight. In our summer this is reversed. Above $66\frac{1}{2}°$N the Sun is above the horizon for 24 hours a day.

Due to the fact that it is twilight until the Sun is 12° below the horizon it is never really dark on midsummer day above $54\frac{1}{2}°$ N. Narvik is in Lat. 68°N, well inside the Arctic Circle as the parallel of $66\frac{1}{2}°$N is called, and in this country Whitby, Darlington and Whitehaven are all in Lat. $54\frac{1}{2}°$N.

In the extreme north of England in midsummer, and the whole of Scotland in June and July, it never really gets dark, and the further north you go the longer the daylight lasts. One thing the Scots are lavish with in summer is their daylight. I have a licence to say this kind of thing, by the way, being one myself.

The moon is a satellite of the earth and is over a quarter of a million miles away. It goes round the earth in an easterly direction on a plane tilted about 5° from the plane of the earth's orbit round the sun.

This gives the moon a maximum declination of about 29°. It takes $27\frac{1}{2}$ days to go round the earth, but due to the earth's movement round the sun there is a period of 29 days between each new moon.

This is called a lunation – or what the Red Indians used to call a "moon", which was a very convenient time interval, though short.

New moon occurs when the sun and moon are in line with the earth and when they are on the same side of the earth.

Fig. 2.

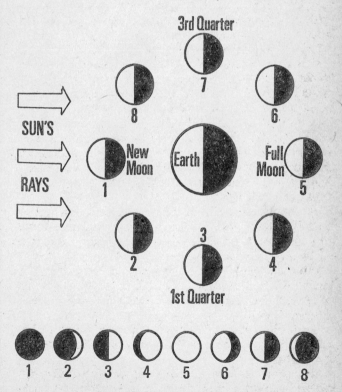

Fig. 3.

111

Full moon when they are all in line, but when the sun and moon are on opposite sides of the earth. Diagram (Fig. 3) will show how the different phases of the moon are caused.

The row of moons along the bottom show how it appears from the earth in 50°N Latitude when at the corresponding numbers on the orbit diagram.

The new moon rises and sets at the same time as the sun and the full moon rises at sunset and sets at sunrise. It rises about 50 minutes later each day, and since it affects the tides, this is why every High Water is about 25 minutes later than the one before, and why High Water tonight is about 50 minutes later than the one last night.

An interesting fact is that the moon turns on its axis in the same period of time that it takes to go round the earth, and so we always see the same side of it. It also makes a moon day equal to 28 of our days, with a period of 14 days sunlight followed by 14 days night – a long day's night.

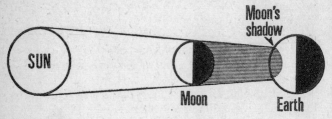

Fig. 4.

Eclipses of the sun are caused by the moon getting between us and the sun at new moon. Not at every new moon, because of the 5 deg. difference between the earth's orbit and the moon's orbit. There are at least two eclipses of the sun every year, but they are not visible everywhere and so to the ordinary observer they are rare.

Actually they are more frequent than eclipses of the moon. The diagram (Fig. 4) shows how an eclipse of the sun occurs.

Sometimes the moon is so far away from us that its shadow does not reach the earth, and in that case the rim of the sun can be seen round the moon. This is called an annular eclipse.

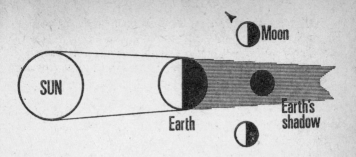

Fig. 5.

Eclipses of the moon are caused by the earth getting between it and the sun, at full moon, as shown.

And that's about it. I have in a couple of thousand words explained the working of the universe to you as far as we know it. For this explanation we are indebted to the work of astronomers for hundreds of years, and particularly from Galileo onwards, until now we can purchase a book called the Abridged Nautical Almanac which gives the position of the sun, moon, four planets, and about 150 stars for any time of the year, in relation to the Greenwich meridian and the equator.

This is both useful and wonderful, and we give them every acknowledgement for this information.

For our picture of the universe, however, we are going to dispense with reality and go back to an astronomer called Claudius Ptolemaeus, Ptolemy for short, a simple, straightforward type of man with a sense of his own importance, who lived during the second century A.D. in Alexandria.

Ptolemy looked up into the sky and saw the sun come up in the East and set in the West, and not only the sun but every other visible heavenly body also. He therefore came to the conclusion that the earth was the centre of the universe and that all these bodies went round it to the Westwards, in circles and at different distances from it.

We, being the same type of men as Ptolemy; to wit, simple, straightforward, and with a sense of our own importance, look up into the sky, see this happening, and agree with him. He was right. This is the man for us, for this conception of the celestial goings-on is much easier for us to understand.

It is called the "Apparent Motion" of the aforesaid bodies, for now we know better than Ptolemy, that it is not truly their "Real Motion".

CHAPTER TWENTY-TWO

DETERMINING NOON

When the sun rises in the East every morning its distance above the horizon continues to increase until it culminates at noon. This distance above the horizon is called its "altitude", and it culminates when it gets to its maximum altitude.

In Britain, as the altitude increases so the sun gradually works its way round towards the South point of the horizon, and when it reaches its maximum altitude it is bearing due South, or 180 deg. True. This means that it is on the same meridian of longitude as you who are looking at it, and the apparent time is twelve o'clock.

If an observer takes a sextant altitude of the sun at noon, it is possible for him to calculate from it his exact Latitude, and very simply, as you will see. This is what is known as "shooting the sun at noon" among novelists, and "noon sights" among seafarers, and it is widely practised as being easiest and most reliable way of finding the Latitude.

It also ends the day and makes a convenient interval from

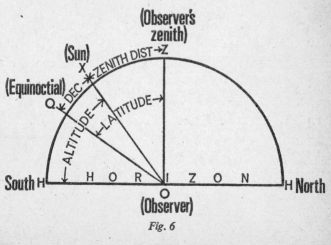

Fig. 6

the previous noon for calculating the distance run, course and speed made good for the day.

The method of determining noon is to check the sun's altitude from about fifteen minutes before noon, when it will increase gradually, hesitate, and begin to go down again. As soon as it starts to drop, check the maximum altitude and make it twelve o'clock.

With this altitude and the declination of the sun taken from the Almanac, the Latitude is found as follows (see Fig 6):

This figure is on the plane of the observer's meridian. We are looking at him from the East point of the horizon but from an infinite distance away, and directly above him is his Zenith (Z). The sun at noon is at "X" on the same meridian and bearing South. "Q" is the point where the equator produced into space cuts the meridian and "QX" is the declination of the sun.

XH is the sun's altitude, and if we subtract this from 90 we get the Zenith Distance (ZX), for ZH = 90.

By adding this Zenith Distance to the Declination we get ZQ, the distance from the zenith to the equinoctial, which is equal to the distance between the observer and the equator, and this is his Latitude. Follow this through carefully on the figure.

In this case the altitude of X is 52°S. The Declination is 19°N. Let us work out the Latitude.

True Alt.	52°S
	90°
*Zen. Dist.	38°N
*Declination	19°N
Latitude	57°N

*Same names add, Opposite names subtract.

The altitude is always named the same as the bearing of the sun from the observer, and the Zenith Distance for the direction of the Zenith from the body.

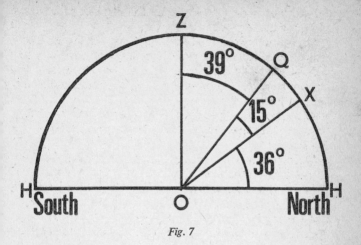

Fig. 7

This is confusing, and I intend it to be because I want to avoid giving you the rules for naming the latitude, which are even more confusing. Instead, I want to encourage you always to draw a diagram, even a rough one, like the one shown above and from it to see whether to add or subtract the Zenith Distance and Declination, and how to name the Latitude.

Let us take another example. At noon to an observer the sun, bearing North had a True Altitude of 36° and a Declination of 15°N. Find the observer's Latitude (see Fig. 7).

True Alt.	36°N
	90°
Zenith Dist.	54°S
Declination	15°N
Latitude	39°S

Easy, isn't it? I feel like a traitor giving away a trade secret, because that is all there is in finding the Latitude at noon. Well, not quite, but that is the principle of it, and we will go into the refinements later.

In the meantime draw figures for the following questions and find the observer's Latitude in each case.

(1) True Alt. 80°S, Decl. 20°S.

(2) True Alt. 22°S, Decl. 23°S.

(3) True Alt. 49°N, Decl. 1°S.

Answers at the end of the chapter.

This is called finding the Latitude by a meridian altitude, and the principle is the same whatever the body – sun, moon, planet or star. The sun comes on the meridian at noon, but the time at which the others come on the meridian varies. In the case of the moon, by day it can be observed to culminate in the same way as the sun, by keeping a check on the altitude until it begins to decrease.

The planet Venus can also be seen through a sextant in the daytime when it is at its farthest distance East or West of the sun, that is, when its elongation is greatest. But the time of its passage across the meridian, and its approximate meridian altitude, must be worked out before it can be picked up.

The only time stars may be observed using the sea horizon is at twilight, when both the stars and the horizon are visible. This period varies in different parts of the world and lasts usually from ten to twenty minutes. The chances of a navigational star being on the meridian at either morning or evening twilight are very slight, though of course it does happen.

Altitudes cannot be measured in the dark except by using a bubble sextant or an artificial horizon. The latter consists of a small dish of mercury covered by a thing like a garden cloche which keeps the wind from ruffling the surface. The dish must be kept fairly steady so this kind of horizon is no good on a lively boat.

Other artificial horizons can be made by using a plate of black treacle, or black oil, and a mirror can be used, too, but this must be set up exactly level, which is quite difficult, and only possible on shore.

To use an artificial horizon the object is brought down by the sextant to its reflection on the reflecting surface, whatever it is, and this measures twice the altitude required, except for a few minor corrections which I will detail later.

Answers: (1) Lat. 10°S, (2) Lat. 45°N, (3) Lat. 42°S.

CHAPTER TWENTY-THREE

KNOWING THE SEXTANT

In order to measure the altitude of any celestial body we must use a sextant. A new sextant can cost from £60 upwards, and a secondhand one from about £20. There is a plastic model now on the market costing about £4 and reading to 1' of arc, which is not bad. At the price one cannot expect too much. Let me say, however, that it is value for money.

I can suggest a substitute for most things and even give instructions for making certain useful appliances for navigational purposes, but there is no substitute for a sextant, nor can I recommend a home-made one.

There is nothing complicated about a sextant. Anybody can use one after an hour's practice and can learn to adjust it in another hour with a bit of application. It is this latter process that I want to explain now.

The photograph shows the principle parts of the sextant and is self explanatory.

When taking an altitude the light from the body strikes the index mirror and is reflected on to the horizon mirror, which is half mirror, half clear glass. It then reflects to the observer's eye which sees the horizon through the horizon glass at the same time.

The index bar is adjusted so the body touches the horizon and the index will then show it's altitude.

To enable the altitude to be taken with accuracy the sextant must be correctly adjusted. This adjustment is done when the sextant is first acquired and should not need doing again unless the instrument is dropped or knocked.

It is a bad policy to be always fiddling with the adjustment screws as they become loose and go out of adjustment at a touch.

At one time seafarers would have their sextants adjusted and then encourage the screws to rust up so that they would not move and spoil the adjustment.

This was done by applying simple corrosives such as brine from the salt beef barrel, lime juice, or plain salt water, but this is going to the other extreme. It is better simply to adjust the sextant and leave it.

There are three adjustments. The first is to set the index mirror perpendicular to the plane of the sextant.

This is done by holding the sextant flat with the arc away from you and with the index about half-way along the arc. Look into the index mirror at the reflection of the arc and at the same time look past the mirror to the true arc. The true and reflected arcs should appear continuous. If they do not, turn the screw at the back of the mirror until they do. Figs. (8a) and (8b).

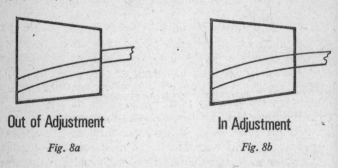

Out of Adjustment   In Adjustment

Fig. 8a   *Fig. 8b*

The second adjustment is to set the horizon mirror perpendicular to the plane of the sextant. This time set the index at about zero, hold the sextant flat and look through the telescope and horizon mirror at the horizon.

The reflection of the horizon and the horizon outside the glass should be continuous. If they are not, turn the adjustment screw which is farthest away from the sextant at the top of the horizon mirror until they are. Figs. (9a) and (9b).

The third adjustment is to set the horizon mirror parallel to the index mirror when the index is at zero.

With the index set at zero exactly hold the sextant vertically and look at the horizon. The true and reflected horizons in the horizon glass should be continuous. If they are not, turn the adjustment screw at the back of horizon mirror,

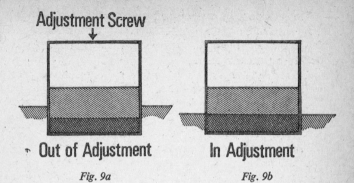

Adjustment Screw

Out of Adjustment   In Adjustment

Fig. 9a   *Fig. 9b*

the one nearest the sextant this time, until they are. Figs. (10a) and (10b).

For those who are land-locked and do not have a sea horizon readily available the second and third adjustments can be made using a star.

This method has several advantages. You can see stars from anywhere, the stars are so far away that the adjustment is not affected by sextant parallax, and the two adjustments can be done holding the sextant in the one position.

Having completed the first adjustment as already explained, to adjust the sextant by means of a star set the index exactly at zero. Hold the sextant vertically and look through the telescope at any bright star. The true and reflected stars will be seen in the horizon mirror, probably one above and to

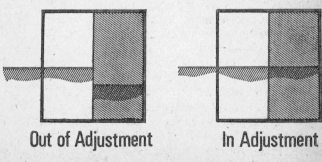

Out of Adjustment   In Adjustment

Fig. 10a   *Fig. 10b*

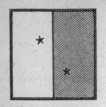  

Before Adjustment **2nd Adjustment** **3rd Adjustment**
         completed   **completed**

Fig. 11a   *Fig. 11b*   *Fig. 11c*

one side of the other. By turning the second adjustment screw the true and reflected stars are brought into line vertically. By turning the third adjustment screw they are brought together when only one star will be seen. The sextant will then be in adjustment. Figs. (11a), (11b) and (11 c).

Having adjusted the sextant do not touch the adjustment screws again. If, on running through the adjustments at any time, you find that the sextant is out, then of course, you will have to re-adjust it, but this is very unlikely.

It may be, however, that a very small error may creep in, called index error.

This is discovered by holding the sextant vertically and looking at the true and reflected horizons, or a star.

This time bring the horizon into line or the stars together by turning the tangent screw. The reading on the sextant will then be the index error. If the reading is on the arc it must be subtracted from every altitude, but if it is off the arc, i.e., below zero, it must be added.

"If it's on take it off, if it's off put it on." There may be no index error.

CHAPTER TWENTY-FOUR

VERTICAL ANGLES

Having discovered how to adjust the sextant, and at the same time by your own efforts how to read it, I hope, we can now advance to its actual use. It is used to measure vertical and horizontal angles, but as far as astro-navigation is concerned we will confine ourselves to vertical angles.

These vertical angles are measured from the celestial body being observed down to the visible horizon, resulting in an angle called the sextant altitude.

When taking an altitude of the sun it is usual to measure from its lower edge or limb. Undo the clamp screw, set the sextant at zero, hold it vertically and look at the sun, taking care to interpose a few of the upper and lower shades. Push out the index bar and follow the reflection of the sun down, keeping it in the horizon mirror, until it is near the horizon.

Tighten the clamp screw, lift the lower shades, and bring the lower limb of the sun on to the horizon by turning the tangent screw.

In the case of the moon you must always put the complete limb on the horizon as shown, either upper or lower. Figs. (12a), (12b) and (12c). Stars are brought down until the horizon passes directly through them, and in every case the angle on the sextant will be the sextant altitude.

Before this altitude can be used it must undergo several corrections, the first of which is for index error. When index

Fig. 12a   Fig. 12b   Fig. 12c

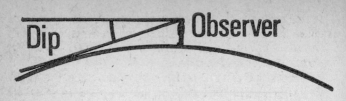

Fig. 13

error is applied (see Chapter 23) we are left with the observed altitude.

The observer's eye-level is always above the level of the visible horizon and the higher the observer is the more of this horizon will be below his eye level. The level through the observer's eye is called the sensible horizon and the angle of depression of the visible horizon below this is called the "dip" of the sea horizon.

This correction can be found for various heights of eye inside the front cover of the Abridged Nautical Almanac and in any of the privately published nautical almanacs or nautical tables. So indeed can all the altitude corrections mentioned in this article.

The dip correction is always negative and should be subtracted from the observed altitude to give the apparent altitude of the body observed.

We are all familiar with the optical illusion by which we see a bend in a stick which is dipped into water. This is caused by the fact that the speed of light is affected by the density of the medium through which it passes, causing it to bend.

Since we see an object in the direction of the ray of light from it as it hits our eye, we see the part of the stick which is immersed in the water to be displaced. It looks bent at the surface.

In the same way a ray of light travelling from the sun to the observer's eye passes through air of ever-increasing density and comes in a curve and not a straight line. This means that the sun we see is not the true sun but one which is slightly displaced and which is always higher than the true sun. Fig. (14). This displacement is the error in altitude due to "refraction" and is listed among the altitude corrections under this heading. Refraction is greatest when the body's altitude is low and zero when its altitude is 90 degrees. This correction is always negative.

The position of large bodies such as the sun and moon is always given for their centres and since we measure the altitude of a limb there is a correction for what is called "semi-diameter". This is the angle at the observer subtended by the body's radius.

This is always added when the lower limb is observed and subtracted from the upper limb. The correction varies slightly throughout the year because the distance of the sun and moon from the earth alters from time to time, and the moon's semi-diameter also increases with altitude because it is close to us to begin with and comes appreciably closer to an observer as it rises in the sky.

This is called the "augmentation of the moon's semi-diameter", augmentation being a high-class term for increase.

Finally, there is parallax. Parallax is caused by the apparent displacement of the body by an actual displacement of the observer and is a widespread phenomenon. One example of it is seen when we look through alternate eyes causing a shift in the scenery.

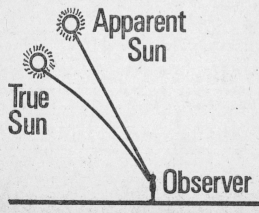

Fig. 14

In astro-navigation parallax is caused by the fact that we take observations from the surface of the earth instead of from its centre. This correction is always added and it decreases as the body's altitude increases, being zero when the body is overhead.

By applying this final correction we reduce the altitude to another horizon passing through the centre of the earth and parallel to the sensible horizon. Fig (15).

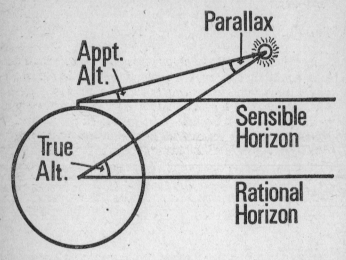

Fig. 15

To correct the altitude of a star or planet only dip and refraction are applied and these two corrections are given separately in the nautical almanacs and together in the nautical tables.

To correct the altitude of the sun all four corrections must be applied and they are given in the nautical almanac, dip on its own, refraction parallax and semi-diameter together. A total correction is given in the nautical tables.

EXAMPLE

Here is a layout for two hypothetical altitudes:

November 5th. The sextant altitude of the sun's lower

limb was 36 degrees 42 minutes and at the same time the sextant altitude of Venus was 40 degrees 27 minutes, height of eye 6 feet, index error 3 minutes off the arc.

Sun		Venus	
Sextant alt.:	36° 42′	Sextant alt.:	40° 27′
Index Error:	3′	Index Error	3′
Observed alt.:	36° 45′.1	Observed alt.:	40° 30′.1
Total corr.:	12′.6	Total corr.:	3′.5
True alt.:	36° 57′.6	True alt.:	40° 26′.5

It will be noticed that the arguments used when entering the main correction table are the height of eye and the altitude of the body, and it is also important when using the sun's total correction to apply the correction for the month given in the small table at the foot of the page in Norie's Tables.

The true altitude must always be obtained before embarking on any position-finding calculations.

CHAPTER TWENTY-FIVE

FIRST CALCULATIONS

Well, now that you can adjust your sextant, take an altitude of the sun and correct it so that it becomes a true altitude, you no doubt want to get on and be able to find out where you are, and this I am going to explain to you as fast as I can.

Let us suppose that you are standing in Greenwich Park by the old observatory on a fine sunny morning. The sun has been climbing up the sky for hours and beside you a sundial shows 12 noon.

The sun is now on the Greenwich meridian and its Greenwich hour angle is zero. As time goes on its hour angle increases, by 15 degrees every hour in fact, so that at 1500 hours sundial time its hour angle is 45 degrees and at 0900 hours the next morning its hour angle will be 315 degrees at our location.

Since we are on the Greenwich meridian this hour angle would be both the Greenwich hour angle and the local hour angle. This hour angle increases from 0 degrees right round the earth as the sun goes west until it comes back again to noon next day when its hour angle would be 360 degrees or 000 degrees as it begins again.

Let us move ourselves now to the south coast of Ireland, to Mine Head Lighthouse, because this lighthouse happens to be in Long. $7\frac{1}{2}$ degrees West. Half an hour after the sun crosses the meridian of Greenwich it crosses the meridian of Mine Head Lighthouse. At this moment the Greenwich Hour Angle (GHA) is 007 degrees 30 minutes, the local hour angle is 000 degrees and the observer's longitude is 7 degrees 30 minutes West.

These three facts are closely linked to each other because with any two you can find the third one, and this is how it is always done: you subtract west longitude from the GHA to get the LHA, i.e., "Longitude West, GHA best". And you add east longitude to the GHA to find the LHA.

For example:

            GHA   160° 47'
            Long   127° 02'W
            LHA   33° 45'

or

            GHA   306° 27'
            Long   47° 51'E
            LHA   354° 18'

A knowledge of this process is invaluable as in solving the navigational triangle which we will do later the LHA is one of the three arguments used to find the parts of the triangle we want to find – the Calculated Zenith Distance and the Azimuth, of which more later.

The Greenwich hour angle of the sun is given in the nautical almanac for Greenwich Mean Time and at hourly intervals. There is a table at the back for interpolating for fractions of one hour which is simplicity itself to use.

Look up the almanac on the date in question using the GMT of the time the sun's altitude was taken. For the nearest hour take out the GHA and, while you are at it, take out the declination also from the adjoining column. Write them both down.

Look up the increment at the back of the almanac for the sun's hour angle with the odd minutes and seconds of time and add this increment or increase to the GHA for the hour. This will give the required GHA.

The sun's declination changes very little in an hour so you can guess the change in it for the odd minutes and seconds but be sure to watch whether it is increasing or decreasing. The declination is another of the three arguments needed in solving the triangle I mentioned. The declination of the sun is the same as the latitude where it would be over head at noon.

The third argument is the assumed latitude. When working out a sight the ship is assumed to be in a position which is estimated as closely as possible. The estimated longitude is used to find the LHA from the GHA and the

LHA, the declination and the estimated latitude are used to solve a triangle.

For navigational purposes you must be able to get the exact GMT to the nearest second at any time. This is done by keeping a very good clock or watch on GMT or as near it as possible. The clock error can be found from radio time signals or by calculation from previous time signals.

In the meantime check your watch by the BBC, wind it at the same time every day, and don't knock it about too much and thereby help it to keep regular time.

Let us now try to visualise the triangle I mentioned previously. This is best done by drawing a figure. The figure I am going to draw is on the plane of the rational horizon, i.e., the plane through the centre of the earth at 90 degrees to the observer's zenith.

Let us assume that the observer's position is 52 degrees N, 14 degrees W, that the sun's declination is 20° N and that the LHA is 045 degrees.

The circle NESW is the rational horizon with Z, the observer, in the centre. We are looking down on the top of his head. Since he is in 52 degrees N the equator will be 52 degrees to the south of him, passing through WQE.

The parallel of declination, dd, will be 20 degrees north of WQE since the declination is 20 degrees N, and the sun will be at X, making the angle ZPX, the LHA, equal to 45 degrees. We join ZX, which is the Zenith Distance, and the triangle PZX is the one we are interested in.

PZ is the latitude subtracted from 90 degrees. PX is the sun's declination subtracted from 90 degrees. ZX we know is the Zenith Distance. Angle ZPX is the LHA. Angle PZX is the azimuth or bearing of the body. Angle PXZ is and outcast and nobody takes any notice of it. It is called the parallactic angle.

We are interested only in the Zenith Distance and the Azimuth in our triangle in that they are the parts we have to find. This can be done by working with natural and logarithmic functions of angles or by looking up books like ready-reckoners. We are going to do both.

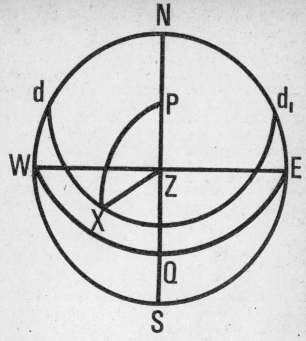

Fig. 16

Do not be put off by a lack of mathematical knowledge or ability before we start our calculations. I have two test questions which, if you can answer correctly, show that you will be able to do all the calculating needed.

Question 1: What is this number? 9. Question 2: How much is two plus two? You think I'm kidding? Not a bit of it.

CHAPTER TWENTY-SIX

CIRCLES OF EQUAL ALTITUDE

A position line is a line drawn on the chart passing through the ship's position. The bearing of a light is a line of position. If we know that we are four miles from a lighthouse then our position line will be a circle drawn round the light with a radius of four miles and so on.

When we measure the altitude of a heavenly body and subtract the corrected altitude from 90 degrees we get the zenith distance, i.e., the distance in arc from the body to the observer's zenith, or if you like, the distance in arc on the earth's surface from the Geographical Position of the body to the observer.

Our position would then be a circle drawn on the earth with centre the G.P. and a radius equal to the zenith distance.

By measuring the altitude of two bodies at the same time and laying off both position circles our position would be at one of the intersections of the two circles. These two circles could cover thousands of miles so there would be little doubt which intersection was the correct one (Fig. 17).

These circles are called circles of equal zenith distance or circles of equal altitude. If they could be drawn on a big enough globe or chart then there would be no difficulty in finding a position but this method is impracticable because of the immensity of such a chart or globe.

However, the problem can be solved by tackling it another way.

Instead of worrying about the G.P. we work out the zenith distance for an assumed position, together with the bearing of the body and compare this calculated zenith distance with the one actually measured.

The difference between them will be the actual distance we are from the assumed position either along the bearing if we are nearer the body than the assumed position, or on

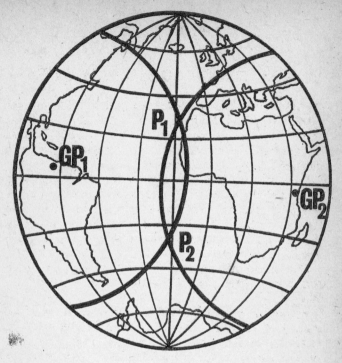

Fig. 17

the reversed bearing if we are further away from the body than the assumed position.

This position at the end of the intercept is called the intercept terminal position and is one position through which the position circle or circle of equal zenith distance passes.

Since this circle is so big the small part of it at the end of the true bearing can be assumed to be a straight line and it can be drawn through the intercept terminal position at right angles to the true azimuth. Here is an example.

From a chosen position of 47 degrees 57 minutes N, 18 degrees 26 minutes W, the calculated zenith distance of a body was 37 degrees 26 minutes, bearing 220 degrees T,

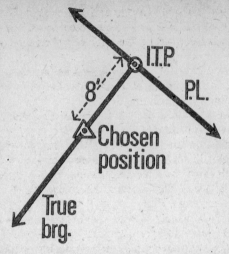

Fig. 18

and the true zenith distance as measured was 37 degrees
34 minutes. It is required to plot the intercept terminal
position and draw the position line through it.

Calc. ZD	..	..	37° 26′
True ZD..	..	..	37° 34′

Intercept   8′ Away

(from the body's G.P.)

This would be drawn on the chart as in Fig. 18.

We will now undertake the solution of the PZX triangle
with the data we are likely to get from an observation of the
sun. This data consists of an estimated position of the ship
in latitude and longitude, the sun's altitude, and the Greenwich Mean Time to the nearest second when the altitude
was taken.

I am going to omit several steps at this point because I
want you to find out the actual arithmetic involved in
getting the answer we want. We have already and will again
cover the subsidiary work necessary to obtain the Local

Hour Angle, the declination, and the correct GMT, and eventually we will do a complete set of work for a fix of position, when we will gather all the pieces and fit them together.

In the meantime let us assume that we are in a position 39° 35'N, that the sun's declination is 23° 14'N, and that the LHA is 4° 05'. See Fig. 16.

For an explanation of this figure see Chapter 25. It is our purpose by means of the information given us to find the side ZX and the angle PZX in the triangle PZX. The basic formula in spherical trigonometry connects the cosine of an angle with the sines and cosines of the three sides, in this case cosine ZX = cosine PZ cosine PX + sine PX sine PZ cosine angle ZPX.

If we use this formula as it is we will be plagued by the fact that the cosines of angles between 90° and 180° are negative.

This fact gives headaches not only to us but to navigators in general and several subterfuges have been tried out to avoid this occasional negative. The latest of these requires the introduction of haversines and for those interested I will try to explain what they are and why they simplify our task.

The versine of an angle is equal to the cosine of that angle subtracted from one or unity. If we divide this versine by two we find we have a value which is zero when the angle is 0 degrees, which increases to unity when the angle is 180 degrees, and which is always positive. Let me show you this on a diagram (Fig. 19).

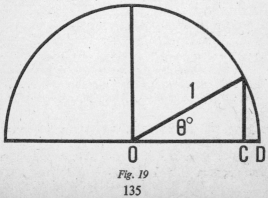

Fig. 19

The radius of this semi-circle is taken to be unity so that the cosine of angle θ degrees (theta) would be the line OC, and 1 — cos θ degrees is equal to CD, the versine of θ degrees. The half of CD is the haversine. It increases at only half the rate of CD as the angle θ degrees increases, so its value will be OD when the angle θ degrees is 180 degrees, i.e., it is unity, and still positive.

By substituting haversine for $\dfrac{1-\cos}{2}$ in the cosine formula we come up with the following equation:

hav a = hav (b ⌣ c) +
sin b sin c hav Â
or hav zx = hav (pz ⌣ px) +
sin pz sin px hav P̂
and for the true azimuth:

hav Ẑ =
$$\frac{\text{hav px} - \text{hav (pz} \smile \text{zx)}}{\text{sin pz sin zx}}$$

There are some of my readers who can follow this exposition and many more I fear who can't. It is the latter group that worries me and I would exhort them not to go away.

We are now over the summit and from now on all we will be doing is practical work not entailing any more theorizing and no theoretical knowledge will be necessary to find the answers we require from our workings.

The important things to understand are the theory of position circles outlined at the beginning of the next chapter and the fact that we calculate the zenith distance of the selected body for an assumed position which only need be approximate.

By comparing this calculated zenith distance with the one we measure we can find by their difference how many miles the assumed position is from one position on the position line, and finally that for a definite fixed position we need two position lines.

One more modification to the Haversine Formula and we are all set to go. If we look again at it in this form:

Hav. ZX = Hav. P sine PZ sine PX + Hav. (PZ~PX) and remember that PZ is the co-latitude and PX the polar distance or co-declination then instead of sin PZ and sin PX we can substitute cos latitude and cos declination respectively, and (PZ~PX) becomes (latitude~declination).

This sign ~ means "difference between" and really means that we find the angular distance between our own parallel or latitude and the parallel of the body's declination.

If the latitude and declination have the same name, north or south, they must be subtracted, and if they are of opposite names they must be added. Now we can write out the Haversine Formula in its final form:

Hav. Zenith Distance = Hav. P cos latitude cos declination + Hav. (Latitude ~ declination).

I would now like to lead you through a complete calculation, explaining each step as we come to it. I am using a 1958 Almanac for this example but later when using the pre-computed tables we will come more up to date and use the 1967 Almanac.

On Jan. 2, 1958 at approximately 1600 hrs ship's mean time in an assumed position 15°25′N, 41°01′W the sextant altitude of the sun's lower limb was 17°16′.5, index error 2′ off the arc, height of eye 59 ft., correct GMT 18h 58m 52s. Calculate the intercept and the direction of the position line.

From the almanac, using GMT January 2 at 18h 58m 52s:

Greenwich Hour Angle for 18h ..		..		..	88° 58.5′
Increment for 58m 52s ..		..		..	14° 43′
GHA ..	..	..	..	..	103° 41.5′
Long West..	..	..	..	..	41° 01′
Local Hour Angle (P̂) ..		..		..	62° 40.5′

Declination for the same Greenwich
| Time is | .. | .. | .. | .. | 22° 54.6' S |
| Latitude | .. | .. | .. | .. | 15° 25' N |

(Lat. ∼ Dec.) .. .. 38° 19.6'

Let us now draw a figure (Fig. 16) before beginning the calculation. This figure was explained in Chapter 25.

P̂ = 62° 40.5' Log. hav.	..	..	..	..	9.43214
Lat. = 15° 25' N Log. cos.		..	..	..	9.98409
Dec. = 22° 54.6' S Log. cos.	..	..	..	9.96432

Log. hav. .. 9.38055

Nat. hav. .. 0.24019
(Lat. ∼ Dec.) 38° 19.6' Nat. hav. 0.10775

Calc. Zen. Dist. 72° 17.6' Nat. hav. 0.34794

| Sextant Altitude | .. | .. | .. | .. 17° 16.5' |
| Index error | .. | .. | .. | .. + 2.0' |

| Observed Altitude | .. | .. | .. | .. 17° 18.5' |
| Dip for 59 ft. | .. | .. | .. | .. — 7.5' |

| Apparent Altitude | .. | .. | .. | .. 17° 11' |
| Main corr. | .. | .. | .. | .. + 13.2' |

| True Altitude | .. | .. | .. | .. 17° 24.2' |
| | | | | 90° 00' |

True Zenith Dist.	..	..	..	.. 72° 35.8'
Calc. Zenith Dist.	..	..	..	.. 72° 17.6'
Intercept	..	..	..	.. 18.2' Away

To calculate the azimuth or bearing of the sun.

Hav. $\dot{Z}$ = [hav. PX — hav. (PZ $\sim$ ZX)] cosec PZ cosec ZX.
Decl.   22° 54.6' S
         90° 00'
_____

PX   112° 54.6'
_____

Lat.	..	15° 25' N
		90° 00'
PZ	..	74° 35'
ZX	..	72° 17.6'
PZ $\sim$ PX		2° 17.4'

PX = 112° 54.6' Nat. hav.	..	..	..	0.69464
(PZ $\sim$ PX) = 2° 17.4' Nat. hav.	..	..	..	0.00040
		Nat. hav.	..	0.69424
		Log. hav.	..	9.84150
PZ = 74° 35' Log. cosec	..	..	..	10.01592
ZX = 72° 17.6' Log. cosec	..	..	..	10.02108
Azimuth N 120° 47½'W Log. hav.		..	..	9.87850

Here we see the advantage of the Haversine Formula over the Cosine Formula – no negative signs and we have an azimuth of 239° 12'.5 without too much nail biting.

The result we have found would be plotted on the chart as shown in Fig. 20.

It is not always convenient to plot the results of sights on the chart, in fact, it is not desirable as charts are precious and the less put on them the better. It is better to use graph paper and to draw the figure to a selected scale of say 1/10 in. = 1 mile or minute of latitude.

There is a complication here. While it is quite easy to find the latitude of the intercept terminal position by measur-

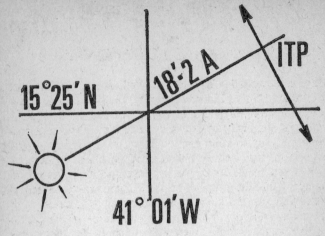

15°25' N   18'·2 A   ITP

41°01' W

Fig. 20

ing the distance it is north of the assumed latitude, the east-west distance of the ITP from the assumed longitude is in miles and is called "departure". These miles must be converted to minutes of longitude.

Difference of Longitude = departure x Sec. latitude, so add the log of the departure to the log secant of the latitude and this will give you the log of the difference of longitude, which must be applied to the longitude of the assumed position.

This can be done by using a table given in nautical tables call the Traverse Table, and a look at the explanation given to this table will soon show how departure can be converted to difference of longitude, and indeed vice versa, without any calculation.

In the next chapter I hope to show you how to combine the results of observations by plotting them on graph paper. This is much the most important part of the whole operation of position finding and, by a stroke of good fortune, the simplest, because you can see what you are doing and position plotting becomes child's play.

CHAPTER TWENTY-SEVEN

WHERE THE LINES CROSS

Have you ever fallen off a horse? Well, as you can imagine, everything is in your favour, gravity, the horse, and, if you can't ride very well, you. It's easy, in fact, it has become a by-word for simplicity of execution. But it's painful either to your body or to your dignity. Now we are going to plot a position just as easily, but painlessly and with dignity.

We have seen how to plot a chosen position, lay off an intercept, and draw a position line. If you take an observation of two bodies at the same time then you lay off both intercepts and draw in the two position lines. If you are on each PL and on both, then you can only be where they cross. Let's take an example,

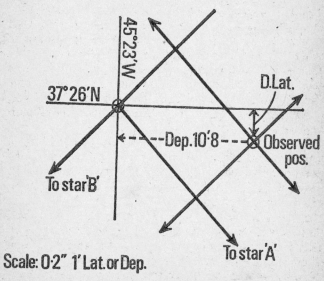

Fig. 21

Just after sunset in a chosen position of 37°26'N, 45°23'W an observation of star "A" bearing 135° gave an intercept of 9' Towards. At the same time an observation of star "B" bearing 225° gave an intercept of 6' Away. Plot the intercepts and position lines and find the position of the vessel.

Select any point as the chosen position and mark the vertical line distinctly with the longitude and the horizontal line with the latitude of that point. From this point draw a line in a direction of 135° and measure 9' along it.

This will be the I.T.P. of star "A". Through this ITP draw a line at right angles to the 135° bearing. This will be the position line given by the observation of star "A". Do the same with the bearing and intercept of star "B". (See Fig. 22).

From the figure the D. Lat. is 1.8S so the observed latitude will be 37°26'N − 1.'8 which is 37°24'.2N. The departure is 10.'8E and converting this into D. Long. by either 10.'8 sec. M. Lat. i.e. 10.8 sec. 37°25' or by traverse table we get a D. Long. of 13.'6E so the observed longitude will be 45°23'W—13.'6 which is 45°9.'4W.

When using pre-computed tables it is necessary to alter the chosen longitude for each observation to make the local hour angle a complete degree. For instance, say the chosen longitude was 26°16'E and the GHA was 047°39'. To make the LHA a whole degree the chosen longitude must become 26°21'E giving an LHA of 074°.

This may look like a bit of a wangle but within fairly wide limits it does not matter what chosen position you use for an observation as long as you plot it and draw the bearing and intercept from it. Let us take another example, Fig. 22.

Just before sunrise in chosen position 23°36'S, 41°27'E an observation of star "A" bearing 052° gave an intercept of 7'T, using long. 41°38'E and an observation of star "B" bearing 320° gave an intercept of 10'T using a long. 41°52'E. Plot the intercepts and position lines and find the position of the vessel.

First plot the longitude for each observation, on the chosen latitude. Draw in the bearing, intercept and position line for star "A" then do the same for star "B" and the posi-

142

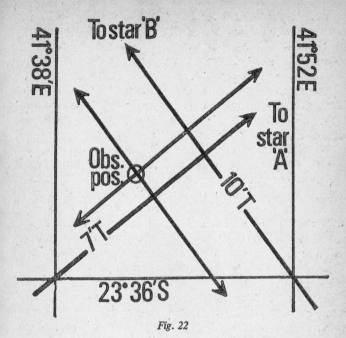

Fig. 22

tion of the vessel will be where the two position lines cross (Fig. 23).

Chosen Lat.	230°36′S	Chosen Long.	41°27′E
D. Lat.	06′N	D. Long.	16′E
Obs. Lat.	23°30′S	Obs. Long.	41°43′E

Notice, by the way, that the only time it is possible to observe stars with a sextant, unless you are using a bubble sextant or an artificial horizon, is at twilight, just before sunrise or just after sunset when you can see both the stars and the horizon at the same time.

By day very often the only body visible is the sun and since it is impossible to get a position from one observation only we combine two observations by running one up to the other, i.e. a forenoon sight combined with a noon sight, a noon sight combined with an afternoon sight, or a forenoon sight combined with an after noon sight.

The interval between the sights depends on the difference between the bearings at the two times. The ideal difference in the bearings is 90°, which gives the position lines a 90° cut as in Fig. 22.

This gives maximum accuracy and this accuracy dwindles as the angle of cut becomes more acute. I think I would put the minimum angle at 20° and be suspicious of it even then.

I would be happier with 40°, but of course something is better than nothing and sometimes you have to be content with what you can get. In the next chapter I will show you how to combine two observations of the same body with an interval between them.

CHAPTER TWENTY-EIGHT

THE END OPERATION

Let me repeat that the most important part of astro-navigation is the plotting of the position lines once obtained. Not only is this the end operation but it is the one in which you can see what you are doing and begin to understand just how the position is arrived at.

Let me take your mind back to the circle of zenith distance drawn on the earth round the Geographical Position of the observed body, Sun, Moon, star or planet, to how this circle is so big that we can consider any small part of it a straight line.

The small part at the observer is the observer's position line, this line being the nearest we can get to a fix from any one observation. To find where this line is we start with any chosen position, work out the bearing and zenith distance of the body from this position, and then compare the zenith distance of the body as actually measured with this calculated zenith distance, the difference being the intercept, or distance the position line is away from the chosen position.

Now let us do some more plotting, this time using the sun. In latitude 46 deg. 25′ N, longitude 26 deg. 47′ W by dead reckoning, an observation of the sun bearing 137 deg. T gave an intercept of 7′ Away. The vessel then ran for four hours at 5 knots on a course of 254 deg. T, when the latitude by meridian altitude of the sun was 46 deg. 22′ N. Find the vessel's noon position. (See Fig. 23).

First plot the chosen position, through this position draw the sun's bearing and measure the intercept 7′ Away from the sun to the Intercept Terminal Position. Through this ITP draw the position line at right angles to the bearing. From the ITP draw the course and distance run and transfer the position line through the end of the run.

Now, always to scale, draw in the parallel of the ob-

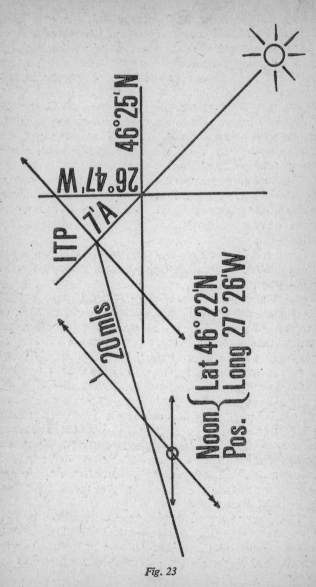

Fig. 23

served latitude. Where this parallel cuts the transferred position line will be the noon position. Remember that the East-West distance between the chosen position and the noon position measured in miles (Departure) must be converted to difference of longitude to get the correct longitude.

This then is the pattern for all observations taken with an interval between them. First, plot the chosen position, the intercept and position line. Lay off the course and distance steamed from the ITP and transfer the position line through the end of the run.

Then plot the chosen position for the second observation, lay off the bearing and intercept of the second body, draw in the second position line, and where it cuts the transferred position line is your position at the time of taking the second observation.

I told you it was easy. I'll do it again, and this time, when you do it, don't look at the figure until after you have completed yours.

In a chosen position of 14 deg. 26′ S, 157 deg. 10′ E at 1000 hours ships' mean time an observation of the sun bearing 062 deg. T gave an intercept of 6′ Towards. After steaming for four hours at 5 knots on a course of 343 deg. T a second observation of the sun bearing 302 deg. T gave an intercept of 5′ Away. Find the vessel's position at the time of taking the second observation. (See Fig. 24).

I would say that the figure is self-explanatory. Notice this time that, having transferred the first position line through the end of the run, this position has been used as the chosen position for the second observation, but indeed the chosen position can be anywhere. As you move the chosen position about before you start the calculation the intercept will change accordingly and always give the position line in the same place.

If you have followed these four examples through you should by now be fairly conversant with the actual plotting of your results. We have already seen how these results are obtained by the Haversine formula and I promised to

147

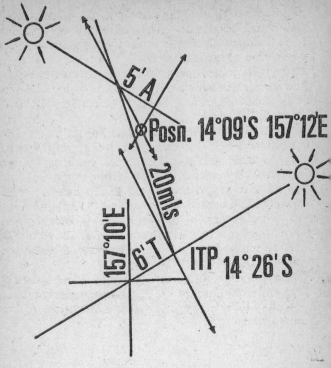

Posn. 14°09'S 157°12'E

5' A

20mls

157°10'E

6' T

ITP 14°26'S

Fig. 24

show you how to get the same results with hardly any working. This I will now proceed to do.

You will remember that when using the Haversine formula to find the calculated zenith distance we first had to have the correct GMT for the time of taking the observation. With this time we extracted from the Nautical Almanac the declination of the body of its Greenwich Hour Angle.

This latter we converted to Local Hour Angle by applying our Longitude and then with Latitude, LHA and Declination we worked out the zenith distance and the body's true bearing.

At some time someone has seated themselves and worked out the zenith distance and true bearing for every combination of Latitude, Declination and LHA and the answers are incorporated in a number of large volumes.

Extracts have been taken from these volumes and published by Her Majesty's Stationery Office in three volumes called "Sight Reduction Tables for Air Navigation," A.P. 3270, Vols. 1, 2 and 3.

Though these volumes as the name implies were meant for use in the air they are just as effective in a ship. Volume 1 covers selected stars for all Latitudes, ensuring a choice of seven stars for observation from wherever you are.

Volume 2 covers all bodies with Declinations up to 29 deg. and all Latitudes up to 39 deg., Vol. 3 all Declinations up to 29 deg. and Latitudes to 89 deg. This covers all that anyone is likely to need, at a total cost of £3 12s. 6d. Vol. 1 should be renewed every 5 years, but Vols. 2 and 3 are permanent.

These volumes together with a current Nautical Almanac, a clock and a radio are all that the navigator needs to cover any or all of the seven seas. I will now demonstrate the use of these tables.

CHAPTER TWENTY-NINE

THEORY INTO PRACTICE

The proof of the pudding is in the eating, so let us collect our cutlery and go. Let us begin with two observations of the sun taken with an interval between sufficient to give us a fairly large difference in bearing, using Volume 3, A.P. 3270 and the Nautical Almanac for 1967. We are in the middle of the Atlantic bound for America in a small ketch.

The date is April 22 in D.R. position 42°17′N, 27°22′W, GMT 10 h. 26 m. 32s. Height of eye 7 ft. Observed altitude of the sun's lower limb 36°39′. Find the intercept and position line.

Using the Nautical Almanac:

Obs. Alt.		36°39′
Dip	—	2′.6
		36°36′.4
Corr.	+	14′.7
True Alt.		36°51′.1
GHA		
Sun 10 h.		330°20′.8
Incr. 26 m. 32 s.		6°38′
GHA		336°58′.8
Long W	—	27°58′.8
Local Hour Angle		309°00′
Declination		12°1′.8N
Corr. for 26 m. 32 s.	+	0′.4
Correct Declination		12°2′.2N

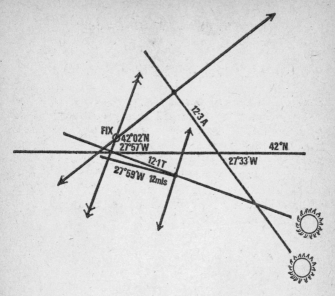

Fig. 25

Looking up page 14 of Vol. 3, A.P. 3270, with the L.H.A. in the right hand column and a declination of 12° at the top of the page, the declination being the same name as the latitude.

Altitude		36°38′
d. + 41′ Az. 109°		
Corr. for 2′	+	1′
Calc. T. Alt.		36°39′
Obs. T. Alt.		36°51′.1
Intercept		12′.1
		Towards

After running on a course of 286°T for two hours at 6 knots the observed altitude of the sun was 54°31′, height of

151

eye 7 ft., GMT 12 h. 24 m. 48 s., DR position 42°20′N, 27°37′W. Find the vessel's position at the time of taking the second observation.

Working exactly in the same way as before:

Obs. Alt.		54°31′
Dip	—	2′.6
		54°28′.4
Corr.	+	15′.3
True Alt.		54°43′.7
GHA		
Sun 12 h.		0°21′
Increment 24 m. 48 s.		6°12′
GHA		6°33′
Long. W	—	27°33′
LHA		339°
Dec.		12° 3′.5N
Incr.	+	0′.3
Dec.		12° 3′.8N
Azimuth		143°
Alt.		54°52′
Corr. 4′	+	4′
Calc. T. Alt.		54°56′
Obs. T. Alt.		54°43′.7
Intercept		12′.3
		Away

To find our position we now have the following information:
(1) Using a chosen position of 42°N, 27°58′.8W we have

152

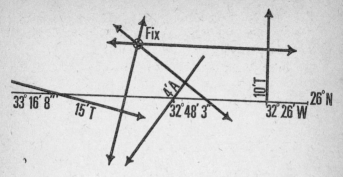

Fig. 26

an azimuth of 109°, and an intercept of 12′.1 Towards.

(2) Using a chosen position of 42°N, 27°33′W, we have an azimuth of 143°, and an intercept of 12′.3 Away.

We must also remember to shift our first position in a direction of 286°T for 12 miles to allow for the run between sights.

Which gives us a position of 42°02′N, 27°57′W.

That the second D.R. position is astern of the first one is due to the fact that the longitude must be adjusted to make the Local Hour Angle a whole degree and doesn't make any difference to the answer.

We will now turn to volume one of the Sight Reduction tables and work out some stars. Stars can only be observed when both star and horizon are visible and this means a rather short period after sunset or before sunrise, though this period can be quite long in high latitudes in summer.

It is intended to observe stars during morning twilight on August 14, 1967 in a D.R. position of 26°24′N, 32°49′W. On looking up the time of sunrise on this day it will be found that the time for sights will be about 0510 ships' time.

S.M.T.	5 h. 10 m.	GHA Aries	67°01′
Long. W +	2 h. 11 m.	Increment	5°15′.9
G.M.T.	7 h. 21 m.	GHA Aries	72°16′.9
		Long. W	−32°49′
		LHA Aries	39°27′.9

Looking up Vol. 1 on page 108 with an L.H.A. Aries of 39° the three stars most suitable for a fix are Aldebaran, Diphda and Kochab. The observations should be set out as follows:

Star	Aldebaran	Diphda	Kochab
GMT	7h 21m 3s	7h 23m 9s	7h 25m 40s
Obs. Alt.	61°17′	37°19′	10°36′
GHA Aries	67°01′	67°01′	67°01′
Increment	5°16′.6	5°48′.2	6°26′.1
GHA Aries	72°17′.6	72°49′.2	73°27′.1
Long. W —	33°17′.6	32°49′.2	32°27′.1
LHA Aries	39°	40°	41°
Azimuth	103°	216°	000°
Calc. Alt.	60°59′	37°19′	10°18′
True Alt.	61°13′.9	37°15′.1	10°28′.4
Intercept.	14.9(T)	3.9(A)	10.4(T)

You will notice from this that it is much easier to work with stars. Now for the plot:

which gives a position of 26°10′N, 32°57′W.

By taking a compass bearing of any body when you measure its altitude you can find the compass error by comparing the True Azimuth with the compass bearing.

Compass bearing of Aldebaran   112°
Compass bearing of T. Bearing   103°
C. Error   9°W

I hope that you have found this book helpful. It could be safely said that the methods described are absolutely the last word in astro-navigation. The next steps are electronic, inertial and satellite navigation. The former needs a lot of apparatus, as indeed they all do, and the two latter I know very little about.

The mantle of Drake, Frobisher and all the pioneer sailors has fallen on you yachtsmen. You are the modern adventurers and in fifty years time when radio controlled ships sail the seas with nobody on board you will be the only people keeping the arts of astro-navigation and seamanship alive. May your voyages all be successful.

APPENDIX

CHAPTER THREE

ANSWERS
Beachy Head
50°44′N, 0°15′E.

Paris Plage
50°30.2′N, 1°35.1′E

Folkestone
51°04.6′N, 1°11.6′E.

Plot
⊕, Mast, ✠ Hope Chapel.

Fixes
(1) 50°58′N, 1°15′E.
(2) 50°50′N, 1°22′E.

CHAPTER FOUR

Folkestone to Dungeness 214°T, 13.3 miles. Dungeness to Royal Sovereign 237°T, 24.8 miles. Royal Sovereign to Beachy Head 268°T, 7.6 miles.

It is possible that you will not get exactly the same answers. If the difference is slight, i.e. 1° in the course and one mile in the distance, don't worry about it.

Remember to measure the distances on the Latitude scale abreast of the course line. It is unlikely that you will be very wrong in this type of exercise, unless of course you find you have gone in the opposite direction and your courses differ from those above by 180°.

CHAPTER FIVE

ANSWERS

PROBLEM 1
   (a) 50°58′N, 1°4′.5E.
   (b) 50°55.8′N, 1°5.2′E.
   (c) Set 172°T, Drift 2.2 miles.

PROBLEM 2
  (a) 51°7.4′N, 1°23.6′E.
  (b) 51°5.5′N, 1°21.7′E.
  (c) Set 212°T, Drift 2.4 miles.

CHAPTER SIX
ANSWERS
PROBLEM 1
  Course 173°T, Speed made good 7.4 knots, Time taken 1 h. 28 m.

PROBLEM 2
  Course 169°T, Speed made good 3.9 knots, Time taken 2 h. 24 m.

CHAPTER SEVEN
ANSWERS
  (1) 051°T, Set 086°T, 5.2 miles.
  (2) 50°52.2′N, 1°5.0′E.
  (3) 50°52.4′N, 1°29.8′E.
  (4) 22°0T, 4.4 miles.

CHAPTER NINE
ANSWERS
  (1) 50°40′N, 0°20′E, 0.4 miles off the Royal Sovereign Lt. V. abeam.
  (2) 51°3.4′N, 1°21′E. 2.7 miles off Dungeness Lt. Ho. abeam.

CHAPTER TEN
ANSWERS
FOLKESTONE TO BOULOGNE
  (1) Folkestone to the Varne Buoy. 119°T, 7.9 miles. 1 h. 36 m. Varne Buoy to Bassure de Baas. 152°T, 15 miles, 3 hrs. Bassure de Baas to R. Canche. 184°T, 14.7 miles. 2 h. 58 m. R. Canche to Treport. 192°T, 29.9 mls. 6 hrs.
  (2) Course 129°T, E.T.A. 0930 (See Chapter 6).
  (3) Course 172°T, 3.7 knots (See Chapter 6).
  (4) Posn. 50°51.7′N, 1°31.6′E, 2.4 miles from C. Gris Nez Lt. Ho. (Chapter 7).

(5) Course 162°T to the Bassure de Baas buoy, 3.2 miles. 172°T to Boulogne Breakwater, 4 miles.

BOULOGNE TO TREPORT
(6) 1 mile.
(7) Set 171°T, Rate 2.32 knots. Course to steer 201°T.
(8) Set 151°T. Drift 2.4 miles, course 215°T. Speed made good 5.4 knots. Estimated Time Arrival (ETA) 1500 hours. The sketch on page 48 explains the answers.

CHAPTER ELEVEN

ANSWERS

Compass Errors 16W, 3E, 8W, 6W, 5W, nil.
Compass Courses 278°, 313°.
Magnetic Courses 195°, 211°.

ADDITIONAL EXCERCISES

ANSWERS

(1) 113°.6′C. 7.8 mls. 146°3′C. 51.7 mls.
(2) Lat. 50°40′.6N, Long. 0°21′.9 E.
(3) Lat. 50°46′.4N, Long. 0°30′.8E. Set 089°T. Drift 2.7 mls.
(4) 074½°C. Bearing 049°T, 7.2 mls. off.
(5) Lat. 50°50′.2N, 0°48′.8E. Deviation 3°W.
(6) 048°C, 12.2 mls. 081°C, 11 mls.
(7) Bearing 292°T, 2.3 miles off.
(8) 200°C, E.T.A. 1110 hrs.
(9) Lat. 50°55′.8N, Long. 1°34′.6E, Set 039°T, Drift 2.3 mls.
(10) Lat. 50°58′.4N, Long. 1°40′.4E. Deviation 6°E.
(11) 156°.7′C. 14.2 mls, 184°.5′C. 15.5 mls.
(12) Lat. 50°47′.6N, 1°34′.8E. Set 120°T. Drift 1¾ ml.
(13) Lat. 51°02′.6N, Long. 1°12′.8E.
(14) 237°C, Bearing 253°T, 8 mls. off.
(15) Lat. 51°00′N, Long, 1°02′.9E.
(16) 260°C. 14.5 mls. 211°C. 10 mls.
(17) 052°C. Distance 6.4 mls.
(18) Set 052°T. Drift 0.9 mls.
(19) Lat. 50°54′.2N, 0°59′.3E.
(20) Lat. 51°03′.4N, Long. 1°20′.6E.

INDEX